Cover:
Giorgio Fossati, *Section of a building of the campo di Ghetto Nuovo*, February 6, 1778, Venice, ASV, *Ufficiali al Cattaver*, b. 277

Editorial coordination
Marco Jellinek

Graphic design
Paola Gallerani

Layout
Arianna Dessì and Chiara Bosio

Printing
BSP Officine Grafiche,
Seggiano di Pioltello (Milan)

isbn: 978-88-99765-29-3
© Officina Libraria, Milan, 2017

Officina Libraria
via Carlo Romussi 4
20125 Milan, Italy
www.officinalibraria.com

Printed in Italy

The translation of this work has been funded by SEPS
SEGRETARIATO EUROPEO
PER LE PUBBLICAZIONI
SCIENTIFICHE

via Val d'Aposa 7 - 40123 Bologna - Italy
seps@seps.it - www.seps.it

Donatella Calabi

VENICE AND ITS JEWS
500 Years Since the Founding of the Ghetto

Translated by
Lenore Rosenberg

OFFICINA
LIBRARIA

TABLE OF CONTENTS

7
FOREWORD

11
CHAPTER ONE: **BEFORE THE GHETTO**
Beginning of the Century, 12 | Usefulness of the Jews, 14 |
Forced Residence, 17 | Foreign Merchants, 19 |
An Example of "Wisdom", 22

25
CHAPTER TWO: **THE "CASTLE OF THE GHETTO"**
The First Island: The Ghetto Nuovo, 26 |
The First Transformations, 29 | New District, New Life, 31 |
Precarious Housing, 33

37
CHAPTER THREE: **THE GHETTO EXPANDS**
A New Place of Refuge: The Ghetto Vecchio, 38 |
1589: A Turning Point, 39 | Frontiers between the Communities, 41 |
The Last Expansion: Ghetto Nuovissimo, 44 |
A Special Legal System, 48

53
CHAPTER FOUR: **PERMITTED TRADES**
Printing and the Spreading of Ideas, 54 |
Moneylending, 59 | Respected Physicians, 62 | Shops and
Brokerage Houses, 63 | Exceptions to the Rules, 65

69
CHAPTER FIVE: **RELIGIOUS LIFE**
Invisible Synagogues, 70 | The Sephardi Appear, 76 |
Not Forgetting to be Venetian, 81

83

CHAPTER SIX: **COMMUNITY LIFE**

Education, 83 | The Obligation to Help, 85 |
The Cemetery at the Lido, 86 | The Canal of the Jews, 92 |
The "New" Cemetery, 94

99

CHAPTER SEVEN: **NAPOLEON DEMOLISHES THE GATES**

The Ghetto is Opened, 101 | Dilapidated Buildings, 103 |
The Gates Are Burned, 105 | An Intermediate Phase, 108 |
The Wind of Modernity, 109 | An Urban Area Like the Others, 113

117

CHAPTER EIGHT: **LEAVING THE GHETTO**

The Great Families Leave the Ghetto, 118 |
Scattered Throughout the City, 126 | A New Generation of
Entrepreneurs, 129 | The Twentieth Century: Integration..., 134 |
... and Disintegration, 136

141

APPENDIX: **TRAVELERS' GLIMPSE OF THE GHETTO**

147

EPILOGUE: **GHETTOS TODAY**

152

ABBREVIATIONS

153

GLOSSARY

159

ACKNOWLEDGEMENTS

March 29, 1516: The Senate decree that required
the Jews to live "together" in the Ghetto

(ASV, *Senato Terra*, March 29, 1516, Reg. 19, fol. 95r)

FOREWORD

On March 27, 1516 the Venetian nobleman Zaccaria Dolfin proposed to the Collegio della Repubblica Serenissima, of which he was a member, that "all" the Jews of Venice be sent to the Ghetto Nuovo, "which is like a castle". Drawbridges were needed, he added, and the area should be enclosed within a wall.[1]

When the Doge informed the "banker Anselmo and other two Community leaders" of the decision,[2] they complained that forcing them to leave shops in the center of the Rialto acquired with huge sums, depriving them of the surveillance guaranteed, and abandoning the traditional meeting places for gentlemen was unjust and would expose them to danger. They ran a high risk of being robbed (*"messi a sacho"*). So, queried Anselmo, how could they assure the Republic the money he guaranteed a few years earlier, money that the Jewish Community had promised to pay? Furthermore—in a tone resembling a threat—his coreligionists might abandon the city for Mestre, where they had previously been forced to live, even though Mestre contained far from enough houses.[3]

Two days later, on March 29, despite the passionate protests of a figure of obvious importance in the negotiations between the government of the Republic and the Jewish Community, the Senate deliberated that "in order to obviate many

1. Gino Benzoni, s.v. "Zaccaria Dolfin," in *Dizionario Biografico degli Italiani,* Vol. 40, Rome: Istituto dell'Enciclopedia Italiana, 1991.

2. On Anselmo and his family and on his role in Venice, see: Brian Pullan, *Rich and Poor in Renaissance Venice,* Oxford: Blackwell 1971, 479–88.

3. Marin Sanudo, *I Diarii,* Venice: 1879-1903, Vol. 22, cols. 72–73, 26 March 1516; cols. 108-109, 5 April 1516.

disorders (*desordeni et inconvenienti*), the Jews of various city neighborhoods were to move "united" to the square of houses located in the ghetto, near San Girolamo.

The Republic chose to set aside an area for the Jewish minority in the city capital. It was limited by two gates that—as the Senate clarified—would be opened in the morning when the marangona (the bell of San Marco's Cathedral that tolled out the rhythm of the city's activities) and closed in the evening by the four Christian guards, paid by the Jews and required to live in situ without families to avoid distractions and exert better control. In addition, two high walls were to be built to close up the area on the side of the surrounding canals, walling up the waterfronts around the boundary.[4] Two boats of the Consiglio dei Dieci with guardians paid by the new "keepers of the castle", were to circulate on the canal around the island to ensure that it was secure.

The following April 1, the same edict was publicly proclaimed at the Rialto and at the bridges of all the city districts where Jews lived.[5]

The decree also affected any Jews who arrived in Venice in the future and was akin to an earlier decision forbidding Jews from staying in the city more than forty days a year. There had already been, in short, several orders aimed at isolating "Jewish perfidy"; now the Jews were permitted to live in Venice to preserve the Christian property pawned in their shops.

---

4. ASV, *Senato Terra*, Deliberazioni, 29 March 1516, Reg. 19, fol. 96r; Sanudo, *Diarii,* Vol. 22, col. 82, 28 March 1516.

5. Sanudo, *Diarii*, Vol. 22, col. 100, 1 April 1516.

To Nicolò, Olivia, Leo, and Giorgio

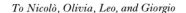

Translator's Note
The names of Venetian magistrates and offices have been left in Italian in the text. Definitions are found in the glossary, which also contains terms relating to names of places and Venetian society.

The location of the three ghettos as seen in
Jacopo de' Barbari's map (1500).

BEFORE THE GHETTO

Pawn broking was in fact one of the Jews' main activities, in Venice as elsewhere in Europe; and perhaps precisely because of this occupation, especially throughout the Serenissima' periods of economic and political difficulties, the acceptance and subsequent settlement of the Jews in the city was justified.[1]

A first agreement between the Venetian government and the Jews on loan management, interest rates and their permanence in the lagoon dates back to 1382. Renegotiated in 1385, the charter was to be renewed every 10 years. But even in 1385 the *Consiglio dei Rogati* (sixty members; founded in the mid-thirteenth century, it was invested with the control of economic affairs, in time assumed all legislative functions and the honorific title of Senate) stipulated an agreement with three moneylenders from Nuremberg—later renewed in 1388—giving them "suitable and sufficient room and habitation" where they could be separated from the others.[2]

The obligation to wear a distinctive sign, a yellow circle on their chest (often not respected) dates back to 1394. In 1496 this obligation was replaced with another, determined by the Senate, of wearing a yellow hat (the bereta zala); this sign changed color over time, but until the arrival of Napoleon, was never completely abandoned.[3] Ten years later (1404), the

---

1. Reinhard Mueller, "Les prêteurs juifs de Venise au Moyen Age," *Annales* 30 (1975): 1277–1302.

2. ASV, *Sopraconsoli dei Mercanti*, 10 October 1388, b. 1, Capitolare, *Liber Quartus Iudeorum*, fol. 64r (reference to the 1385 decision taken by the consiglio dei Rogeti).

3. ASV, *Senato Terra*, 26 May 1496 quoted in David Jacoby, "Les Juifs à

opportunity to live in Venice was drastically limited to no more than two weeks, in an attempt to restrict the banking profession to the sale of unredeemed pawned articles at the Rialto, while other trade was to take place in Mestre. Trade of second-hand objects was only authorized as an alternative.

BEGINNING OF THE CENTURY

Other restrictive measures were taken during the fifteenth century.[4] Especially at the end of the century, after the decrees of expulsion from Spain (1492) and Portugal (1496), migration in the Mediterranean continued. This was even true during periods of political and economic uncertainty for the Serenissima, with the opening of new trade routes to the East and the Americas that heavily influenced the financial needs of its governing body. In this sense, a turning point in authorizing moneylenders to reside in Venice came between 1501 and 1502, when first the Collegio and then the Senate proclaimed that the Jews established in the territories of the Republic could live and carry out their businesses in the city for a period of ten years.[5]

Venise du XIV au milieu du XVI siècle," in Hans-Georg Beck, M. Manoussacas, A. Pertusi, (eds.), *Venezia centro di mediazione tra oriente e occidente (secoli XV-XVI). Aspetti e problemi*, Vol. 1, Florence: Olschki 1977, 175. For the distinctive sign for women see: Benjamin Ravid, "From Yellow to Red, On the Distinguishing Head-Covering of the Jews of Venice," *Jewish History (The Frank Talmage Memorial Volume*, II) 6, nos. 1-2 (1992): 179–210.

4. Jacoby, Les Juifs à Venise, 163–216; Benjamin Ravid, "The Venetian Government and the Jews," in Robert C. Davis and Benjamin Ravid, (eds.), *The Jews of Early Modern Venice*, Baltimore and London: John Hopkins University Press 2001, 3–30. Renata Segre (whom here I thank for having let me see the documents she transcribed), document list concerning Jews in the Archivio di Stato di Venezia (ongoing research).

5. ASV, *Collegio,* Notatorio, 22 December 1501, Reg. 15, fol. 77v; *Senato Terra*, 19 January 1503 (m.v. 1502), Reg. 14, fol. 137v.

Starting in 1508, the *condotta* (or charter, as this form of agreement was called) was renewed in the Venetian territories, granting permission to lending banks for the next five years.[6] As well as setting applicable interest rates, the charter stated that Jews had to rent—and not own—the houses where they lived; but they could also obtain ground elsewhere to bury their dead "as they had at the Lido." Similarly to a deal made in Piran many years earlier (1484), communities on the mainland could have a synagogue and a hotel to welcome foreigners *secundo el consueto*, according to custom.

Later, in 1515, other trades were allowed in: the opening of ten *strazaria* shops (selling fabrics, clothes, and second-hand goods) in the heart of the Rialto market was granted in exchange for a special new loan, the definitive validation of a service provided to the entire city. Marin Sanudo, a meticulous chronicler of the events of these years, affirmed that there were then 500 Jews, women and children, in the city.

"There are many Jews," wrote Marin Sanudo, "in this land, ... in various houses and districts," alluding in different places in his book to San Cassian, Sant'Agostino, San Polo, and Santa Maria Mater Domini. All of these areas were close to the central, international Rialto market, hub of relationships linking the Mediterranean world to western and central Europe.[7] Jews had been able to purchase shops and even some houses in those districts. There was Vivian dal Banco, for example, summoned with his colleague Anselmo to appear before the Doge in March 1516 to hear the decisions of the Collegio. Before the ghetto was established, he lived in the neighborhood of San Bartolomeo, at the foot of the Rialto Bridge, while Anselmo's son lived in Santa Maria

---

6. Pullan, *Rich and Poor*, 476.

7. Sanudo, *Diarii,* Vol. 20, col. 98, 6 April 1515, col. 138, 22 April 1515.

Mater Domini near a nobleman, Contarini, in a *casa da stazio* (a building with apartments to rent) where Jews lived on one mezzanine and a group of prostitutes on another.

USEFULNESS OF THE JEWS

The tendency to live in the city in close proximity already existed; the declarations made to the Dieci Savi alle Decime (the magistrate that collected property taxes) were proof of the discrimination imposed by the Christian owners, as well as a certain amount of speculation on the demand for rentals. At the same time, we should note that "foreigners" were mostly found living in rented residences in the central areas.[8] The *Ufficiali al Cattaver* (the magistrates in charge of public assets) regulated moneylending and Jewish residence in Venice, and—as the Senate later recommended—were to use all their "restraint" to "encourage the merchants of these Nations to quietly continue their trade [...] knowing well the substantial revenues that accrued in our coffers."[9] In actual fact, the approach of Venice in this period was one of uncertainty and inconsistency. There were multiple discussions over the site of the Jews' compulsory residence, with the ultimate aim of creating a physically enclosed space. This was considered a functional solution for control and had already been tested in some of the Venetian sea colonies (on

8. Ennio Concina, "Parva Jerusalem," in Ennio Concina, Donatella Calabi, Ugo Camerino, (eds.), *La città degli Ebrei. Il ghetto di Venezia, architettura e urbanistica*, Venice: Albrizzi 1991, 26, 27 and note 28, 48.

9. Carla Boccato, "Istituzione del ghetto veneziano: il diritto di locazione perpetua o 'jus gazaga' ed i banchi di pegno," *Giornale economico della Camera di Commercio, industria, artigianato e agricoltura di Venezia* no. 3 (May-June 1971): 336–43.
Abram Lattes, *Cenni sulla Comunità israelitica di Venezia*, in *Venezia e le sue lagune*, Vol. I, Venice: Antonelli 1847, Appendix, 103–107; see also ASV, *Ufficiali al Cataver*, 23 December 1516, b. 1, Reg. 2, Capitolare, fols. 125r–126r.

the islands of Crete and Negroponte, the Venetian name for Euboea), and Constantinople, where Jews and Muslims had been allocated a walled district. In particular, some Jews were obliged to live in Pera, on the other side of the Bosphorus strait, but after all they practiced dangerous, smelly or noisy trades (such as dye works).[10]

Moreover, the problem of finding a common solution for the Jews—who were leaving "depressed, for the world" even as they had earlier obtained permission to stay "in this land in great numbers"—had existed since the early sixteenth century.[11] Which is why, even back in 1505, Doge Leonardo Loredan himself allowed two inhabitants of the Jewish faith in Cannaregio to continue managing a hostel to accommodate their fellow citizens; in 1509, after the League of Cambrai and subsequent economic difficulties, he granted a temporary tax reduction to the minority that carried out moneylending activities even though they were unable to pay the usual 14,000 ducats.[12]

After the battle of Agnadello, many Jewish refugees nearby fled to the lagoon. At that time, on the other hand, the same banker Anselmo—who declared a few years later in a petition to the *Avogadori di Comun* (the Municipal Attorneys), regarding a dispute with the Pisani bank, that his only desire was to live "quietly under the shade this illustrious domain"—took it upon himself to recover that amount with all possible speed.[13]

---

10. Benjamin de Tudela, followed by other authors, was the first to speak of it; David Jacoby, "The Jews in the Byzantine economy," in Robert Bonfil et al. (eds.), *Jews in Byzantium*, Leyden: Brill 2011, 229–32. On page 210 it is explained how, paradoxically, the separation within the Pera area was due to existing contrasts between Jews.

11. Sanudo, *Diarii,* Vol. 20, col. 98, 6 April 1515.

12. ASV, *Savi alla Mercanzia*, 18 and 21 April 1505, b. 62, II series, fasc. 165, part 3; *Senato Terra*, 21 February 1510 (m. v. 1509), Reg. 16, fol. 178v.

13. ASV, *Capi del Consiglio dei X*, Notatorio, 12 February 1516 (m.v. 1515), Reg. 4, fols. 101v–102r.

In fact, although the Consiglio dei Dieci had reaffirmed in June 1509 that the Jews and their families were to "stay out of this city of ours," Anselmo and no more than one hundred companions, who "were wont to stay in Mestre", continued in fact to reside where "Our Signoria saw fit."[14]

In 1511 the Senate admitted that "a great many hebrei (Jews)" had gathered in "our" lands, lending the Signoria an essential sum of money. That same year, Marco Loredan, an Avogadore de Comun, allowed Grassin di Moisé to marry and celebrate the wedding in the city according to his customs.

In July 1513 and again two years later, the Consiglio dei Dieci granted, as mentioned, permission to a large number of Jews to open new *strazaria* shops in the houses where they lived scattered in the city, as long as they paid the appropriate fees.[15] The Jews were thus a minority of merchants useful to the town economy. The climate, however, was tense, as Christians competitors did not fail to point out the damage done by those businesses' Sunday opening (according to Jewish law, they were instead closed on Saturdays).[16]

Even in the Republic's capital, this was not the first time that the Serenissima took measures. In 1515 an important political figure, Giorgio Emo, suggested that the Council settle the Jews on the Giudecca, while the two bankers Anselmo and Viviano (the same ones called the following year to appear before the Doge) speculated about establishing Com-

14. ASV, *Consiglio dei X*, Misti, 8 June 1509, Reg. 32, fol. 163v; Sanudo, *Diarii,* Vol. 8, col. 305, 21 May 1509; col. 340, 3 June 1509; cols. 355–56, 5 June 1509; col. 406, 15 June 1509; Pullan, *Rich and Poor*, 478n2.

15. ASV, *Senato Terra*, 28 September 1511, Reg. 17, fol. 113r and verso; *Avogaria de Comun*, Notatorio, 20 November 1511, Reg. 2053/3; ccx, 7 July 1515, Notatorio, Reg. 4, fol. 82v.

16. ASV, *Capi del Consiglio dei X*, Notatorio, 29 March 1515, Reg. 4, fol. 49v; 30 October 1515, fol. 71r; 6 November 1515, fol. 81v; 6 November 1516, fol. 82v.

munity on the island of Murano.[17] This was, in a word, an attempt to impose a move away from the city center with a suburban, perhaps insular, solution which required, however, negotiations with the Jews living in Venice, evidently considered equal partners in the discussion.

FORCED RESIDENCE

Ultimately, economic difficulties went hand in hand with new religious policy. The anti-Jewish watershed that was marked by the creation of the ghetto was determined when a united front arose of some illustrious patricians, and the patriarch Antonio Contarini, who had convened two synods, in 1514 and 1519 respectively. It was buttressed by a campaign of the Inquisition initiated at the same time by the Carmelite Francesco da Lucca, and by the Franciscan Giovanni Maria di Arezzo, the talented preacher Friar Zuan de Pontremolo, Venetian citizen Rafaello Uberti, and hermit Gerolamo da Verona, who preached at the churches of the Frari, San Marco, San Giovanni e Paolo, and San Francesco della Vigna.

Hostility, however, was not targeted only at the Jews. In 1515 the Patriarch in person intervened at a session of the Venetian government to prevent the construction of a Greek Orthodox church requested by the Greek community of Venice, and later ordered seizure of the works of Martin Luther sold by a Venetian bookseller.[18] In fact, in spite of Franciscan preaching and injunctions to leave the city in 1511, it does not appear that the Venetian Jewish community in the city declined in that period; indeed, the number of Jewish citizens rose to about 700 in 1516.[19]

---

17. Sanudo, *Diarii,* Vol. 20, col. 138, 22 April 1515.

18. Concina, "Parva Jerusalem," 24–39.

19. Sanudo, *Diarii,* Vol. 12, cols. 110–111, 9 April 1511; Vol. 22, cols. 108–109, 5 April 1516.

Yet, those who lived "in fear of God"—stated the decree of 1516—could in no way allow the Jews to occupy the
same houses as Christians, freely roam the streets by day
and night, or commit sin with "many vices & detestable and
abominable things." To avoid delays, the Senate ordered
all the houses in the Ghetto Nuovo emptied immediately.
The decision concerned the northeast end of Venice, in the
Cannaregio district where the "Geto," the area where the
residues of the nearby copper foundry were thrown, was
once located. The order was given to empty the houses of
their Christian tenants, and there the Jews would live, paying a rent one third higher than that asked of Christian tenants. Landlords would not be required to pay taxes on this
additional portion. No synagogues were allowed, except in
Mestre, and a curfew was imposed that could be suspended
only for doctors, who were allowed to go out to the sick at
night on condition that they informed the guards of their
movements.

The owners of the ghetto houses, several members of the
Da Brolo family, were also summoned. They had different
reactions to the obligation to free their houses to accommodate new residents.[20] But in July of that year, the population
exchange was a fait accompli.[21] There was animated discussion in the Senate in view of the 1519 ricondotta (charter renewal) (signed in March 1520, more veneto—i.e. according to
the Venetian calendar) when many had spoken out against
the renewal. Instead, in a speech, the prestigious Marco Foscari argueed the need to keep the Jews in the city "in order to
make use of the people and the money for every need of the
State," avoiding the error of the Catholic king who expelled

---

20. ASV, *Procuratia di San Marco de Ultra,* Commissaria da Brolo,
b. 57, fasc. 16-18.
21. ASV, *Senato Terra,* 29 July 1516, Reg. 19, fols. 109v–110r; Pullan,
Rich and Poor, p. 488.

them and forced them to flee to Constantinople, taking with them skills and activities that were used to serve the Turks.[22]

Then in 1527, when the ghetto was already a reality, Gabriele Moro again proposed expelling the Jews, a proposition that the Doge, Andrea Gritti, refused to put to the vote.[23]

FOREIGN MERCHANTS

On the other hand, in the sixteenth century, the Venetian Republic pursued an extended and variously articulated strategy of hospitality for merchants of different nations in different *sestieri*. Venice was "a land roamed by many nations of every language and country," said Francesco Sansovino a few years after the ghetto was created.[24] Efficiency, public order, and morality were goals that this mercantile society, had sought since the previous century with financial and legal instruments, but also gradually by organizing the urban fabric and ways of living, working, practicing ritual, and building trade and cultural links with other minorities. Germans, Greeks, Persians, Albanians, Turks, Armenians, Tuscans, and Lucchesi—whose trading activity was valuable in a city that, like Antwerp or Seville and later Amsterdam, founded its fortune on trade—were accommodated not only for their mercantile role, but also because they contributed to the state budget with the payment of ordinary and extraordinary taxes and import duties. All had been granted physical arrangements, corresponding in turn to different degrees of diffidence, lim-

22. Giuseppe Gullino, "Il discorso di Marco Foscari per la ricondotta degli ebrei a Venezia (3 marzo 1520)," *Archivio Veneto*, 5th ser., 158 (1999): 133–57.

23. Sanudo, *Diarii*, Vol. 16, col. 53, 20 March 1513; Vols. 43–44, coll. 303–306, 29 March 1527; BMV, Ms. It. vii, 244 (=9231).

24. Francesco Sansovino, *Venetia città nobilissima et singolare*, Venice: Domenico Farri 1581, 136b.

itations, or guarantees between distinct groups. Convenience was mutual. *Albergarie* (merchant residences) with the right of abode, to store goods, and self government and, at the same time, a guarantee for the state for constant tax revenues, were in fact attributed to the Armenians in San Giuliano, the Germans (peoples of northern Europe) in San Bartolomeo on the Grand Canal, the Persians to San Giovanni Crisostomo, the Turks in San Matteo di Rialto and then in the palace of San Stae, and the Lucchesi in Rialto Nuovo.[25]

It was such a well-defined tactic by the Republic that when, on a winter night in 1505, the German and Flemish district was destroyed by fire, immediate action was unavoidable. With extraordinary operational decision and capacity compared to the usual methods of urban public works, the Senate approved the reconstruction of the warehouse at its own expense, entrusting the task to the *provveditore del sale* (superintendent of salt) and assigning an even larger area for the new building. The new edifice was a square forum, closed between overlapping arcades and loggias, which opened onto about eighty rooms arranged along the square's perimeter: warehouses and living quarters made available to the German nation. In addition to businessmen, we know that painters (such as Albrecht Dürer), printers and large publishers (as Anton Kolb), and musicians or composers (such as Adriaan Willaert) also lived there.

Although created differently, and much later, the "magnificent" lodgings of the Turks also seemed to refer to a similar type of building. After a series of inquiries to find

25. Donatella Calabi, "Magazzini, fondaci, dogane," in Alberto Tenenti and Ugo Tucci, (eds.), *Storia di Venezia,*Vol. 12, *Il mare*, Rome: Istituto dell'Enciclopedia Italiana 1991, 802–807; Donatella Calabi, "Gli stranieri e la città," in Alberto Tenenti and Ugo Tucci, (eds.), *Storia di Venezia,* Vol. 5, *Il Rinascimento. Società ed economia*, Rome: Istituto dell'Enciclopedia Italiana 1996, 913–46; Benjamin Ravid, "Venice and its Minorities," in Eric R. Dursteler (ed.), *A Companion to Venetian History,* 1400–1797, Leiden: Brill 2013, 449–85.

acceptable collaboration, when the Collegio and Cinque Savi alla Mercanzia finally granted the Ottoman nation the medieval palace overlooking the Grand Canal in the vicinity of San Stae, the renovations adapted the stately home as a residence of a foreign community intended to offer "comfort" to guests and "security" to the Venetians. It was necessary to stem rumors and interference from neighbors and therefore all doors to the outside were closed, and the windows shielded with "*trombe*" (panels) of larch, a clear separation of pathways and separation of the space allotted to the different groups: Asians and those from Constantinople were settled near the rio del Megio, and Bosnians and Albanians towards the *salizzada* (paved road). There had to be a good level of services (water wells, daily cleaning, garbage removal), but above all permanent surveillance was provided by a "faithful guardian" who lived in a separate, self-contained dwelling, tasked "not to let in strangers: women, misfits, Christians and armed men." This duty was to be assigned to a well-known, "most Christian" citizen for generations, to guarantee protection to all.[26]

Whether it was a closed warehouse or a guild, a church, a college, which might have had the right of a group of lodgings (as in the case of the Greeks), the Serenissima's responsiveness towards foreigners who carried out their trade in the islands of the lagoon was clear and yet never divorced from a relatively strict system of controls designed to avert conflict between people with diverse behaviors, habits, and languages.[27]

In later times, several "nations" agreed, and in fact "purchased", the service functions assigned to them by the

---

26. ASV, *Compilazione Leggi*, 27 May 1621, b. 210, fols. 184r–191r.

27. Calabi, "Magazzini, fondaci, dogane," 806–807; Donatella Calabi, "Il ghetto e la città, 1541–1866," in *La città degli Ebrei*, 203–206; Donatella Calabi and Jacques Bottin, (eds.), *Les étrangers dans la ville,* Paris: MSH 1998.

Venetian government. In doing so, they conquered—albeit with varying degrees of restrictions—the right to survival and a certain margin of identification with the city and with a private urban space. Ultimately, for centuries citizens and foreigners carried out their activities in Venice to mutual benefit living side by side but basically separate: under the supervision of the magistrates of the Republic, yet enjoying considerable options for self-government.

AN EXAMPLE OF "WISDOM"

That approach was long heard and celebrated as a symptom of "Venetian" wisdom: on the threshold of the fall of the Republic there were still those who admiringly noted that the "charters" renewed from time to time had never granted the Jews "perpetual stability", that they were never "naturalized", nor called "subjects", and the simple the fact that they were always treated as foreigners, was a brilliant legal solution.[28]

Segregation in designated places was apparently accepted by both Venetians and Jews. In his description of "noble and unique Venice", Francesco Sansovino spoke of "the common quarters of the Jews [...] almost like a true promised land" where they "rested in singular peace" [and] enjoyed this homeland. Even taking into account the pro-Republic rhetoric, the expression used was very strong, denoting the fact that the Jews, or at least some of them, had become "exceedingly opulent and rich" due to trade, and saw Venice as a coveted destination. On the other hand at the same time, they were the object of envy and comparison to other foreigners (the Greeks in particular, but also the Turks), who soon petitioned to the Senate for the same rights as "Jewish

---

28. Marco Ferro, *Dizionario del diritto comune e veneto*, Vol. 5, Venice: Modesto Fenzo 1779, 6.

infidels" and "Armenians heretics."[29] Even among the Jews, however, there were clearly supporters of the Venetian Republic and its system of government: in a certain sense, rabbis, philosophers and politicians as Eliah Capsali, Isac ben Jahuda Abravanel and David de Promis also participated in the construction of the myth of Venice.[30]

It was actually a long, long example of the Middle Ages, when for centurie nd were anything but irrelevant insignificant in allowing the work and the centuries-long stay of the Jews in the lagoon.

29. Sansovino, *Venetia città nobilissima*, 136; Ennio Concina, *Venezia nell'età moderna*, Venice: Marsilio 1989, 81; Paolo Preto, *Venezia e i Turchi*, Florence: Sansoni 1975, 130ff.

30. Benjamin Ravid, "Between the Mith of Venice and Lachrymose Conception of Jewish History," in Bernard D. Cooperman, (ed.), *Studies and Texts in Jewish History and Culture*, College Park: University of Maryland 2000, 151–92.

Guido Costante Sullam, Map of the three ghettos: Ghetto Nuovo
(1516), Ghetto Vecchio (1541), Ghetto Nuovissimo (1633).

(Venice, AM)

2

THE "CASTLE OF THE GHETTO"

So, the area selected for the Jews was in Cannaregio: it was on the edge of the city but not confined to an island in the lagoon (as had initially been suggested). It was characterized by activity and increasing urbanization; it was a "court of houses" surrounded by a canal that made control easier. From the start, the Ghetto Nuovo grew in height around a real "square" (the "court of houses" of the first documents).

The type of settlement was of undeniable importance, due to both the choice made and later development. Its determination was not accidental: not only did it ensure supervision and some security to the Jews, and consequently—as in the case of *fondaci*, large warehouses with living quarters—to Venetian citizens, but also included a collective use of open space around which homes, shops and warehouses could be organized. It was in fact a small 'contrada,' typical of the urban structure of Venice, apparently constrictive and akin to military architecture (a castle with walls and drawbridges, as recalled in the founding act), perhaps similar to the fortress-district of the Arsenale, access to which was barred to anyone without the proper title or permission. It also evoked another neighborhood to which the settlement in the *campo* (square) Ghetto Nuovo was compared: the Lazzaretto (hospital for those stuck with the plague), represented in the Venetian cartography as a complex of buildings arranged around a large four-sided field.

The walls that were planned however were never built, and at least two of the shores (belonging to bankers Anselmo and Abram) were already unwalled in December of that year.[1]

---

1. Marin Sanudo, *I Diarii*, Venice: 1879-1903, Vol. 23, cols. 359–60, 2 Dec.1516.

Inside the area there were three pawnshops, wells, shops and places of storage, spaces for entertainment and, despite the initial prohibition, religious services. Represented in roughly like a porched basin, the number of doors and edges of water grew around this courtyard, beyond the regulations established by the Consiglio dei Dieci, and were opened along the outer perimeter to make the place accessible by boat.[2]

THE FIRST ISLAND: THE GHETTO NUOVO

The area set aside for the Jews, approximately pentagonal in form, had long been privately owned and only by chance showed morphological similarities to squares or what Venetians call *campielli*.[3] Thanks to the initiative of the Da Brolo family, the area was totally urbanized in the years 1459-1465, but on a very different scale from the traditional aristocratic court matrix. To explain the vastness, we can presume that the agglomeration of new homes initially included plans for a centrally located chapel, ultimately never built, a branch of the two existing parish churches in the neighborhood.[4]

The three wells within the campo, where the family coats of arms can still be seen today, were also built by the Da Brolo. For a long time, it was only a grassy island that separated by the *rio* (a small canal) from the elongated strip of land up to the wide canal of Cannaregio. Its urbanization, however, would in fact allow new activities, movement and ex-

---

2. ASV, *Inquisitori agli Ebrei*, 1589–1658, b. 45, fols. 340ff.; *Senato Terra*, 16 November 1624, Reg. 94, fol. 238v; *Ufficiali al Cattaver*, 26 January 1615 (m.v. 1614), b. 2, fol. 25; 15 January 1620 (m.v. 1619), b. 2, fol. 39v; 8 June 1632, b. 242, (6 F r., fols. 169v–171v).

3. Giovanni Caniato, "Il Lazzaretto Nuovo," in *Venezia e la peste*, Venice: Marsilio 1979, 343–62.

4. Concina, *Venezia*, 20.

change between the inhabitants forced to live there. The new owners obtained a right of way on the bridge separating the area from the Ghetto Vecchio and the *fondamenta* (quay) of Cannaregio from Marco Ruzini, the land's previous owner. Later, plans were made to build a new bridge over the Rio di San Girolamo (visible in Jacopo de Barbari's map of 1500).

In the aforementioned view of Jacopo de' Barbari—the first available representation of city locations—the campo of Ghetto Novo was surrounded by two-story houses.

Publicly owned and managed work spaces had existed since the fourteenth century: in particular, there was a copper foundry, probably with fourteen kilns, called *Geto de rame del nostro Comun* (the copper foundry of our city).

It is worth noting that, starting from this first enclosure, the word "ghetto", became a term laden with meaning even in its more distant geographical and chronological variations. In actual fact, the word has nothing to do with segregation, or the Jewish minority. Referring initially to the area of the future Ghetto Vecchio, more than the area that the Senate turned into the enclosure of the Jews in 1516, it bespoke of the lines of wheelbarrows that unloaded (throwing, *gettare*) copper slag from the refining process carried out in the workshop adjacent to the islet of which we are speaking, which became the terrain for smelting waste *(terren del Geto)*.

It must be emphasized here that, from at least the fifteenth century on, when the copper foundry was referred to in numerous archives, in some documents the word *geto* was also used to mean taxation, in particular related to canal excavation and maintenance of canal banks, bridges and Giudici del Piovego ordered taxes collected in all the ghetto districts, and again in 1458 hosts were taxed heavily by Piovego and the Heads of the Seamen "According to custom," while in 1460 the Judges of the Piovego went on daily to check that "those required to do so" paid the *geto* to allow the cleaning of the canals and refurbishment of bridges, wells and roads.[5] Ultimately, the expression might have come to have a double meaning, both the name of the area and the local residents' obligation to pay a tax to the Republic.

What is certain is that, with the arrival of the Jews, many of them of German origin, the soft "g" of Venetian dialect became the hard "g" sound of German.

The "court", in its organization, would shortly become a model for the Jews themselves, to the point that it was used as a prototype in the subsequent creation of the ghetto of Padua (1603) and that of Modena (1633).[6] It was in fact a "field surrounded by buildings" as the historian Marc'Antonio Sabellico called it a few years earlier (1502).[7]

The documents available to us certainly do not speak of architecture. The engraving of Venice of 1677 (anonymous) and the later view by Giovanni Merlo (1696) are among the few in which the *geto*—slag field—(in the first) and the *ghetto* (in the second) are perfectly recognizable and identified by name. While the references are perfunctory, the typological allusion is clear: by drawing a portico at the bottom of the field, the authors apparently did not intend indicate a precise façade, but a degree of uniformity due to the presence on the ground floor of shops and spaces open to the public, meant for residents in the form of their relationship with the square.

Later, the meaning of the word referred to a physical, social and institutional separation that still exists today in many political and geographical contexts, common in some US cities,

5. ASV, *Maggior Consiglio*, Deliberazioni, 22 April 1425, Reg. 22 (Ursa), fol. 68r; *Senato Terra*, 28 June 1458, Reg. 4, fol. 75v; 14 November 1460, Reg. 4, fol. 158v.

6. Donatella Calabi, "Les quartiers juifs en Italie entre XV-XVII siècle, Quelques hypothèses de travail," *Annales. Histoire et Sciences Sociales* 4 (1997): 777–98.

7. Marc'Antonio Sabellico, *Del sito di Venezia città,* Venice 1502 (reprint edited by G. Meneghetti, Venice: Filippi 1985), 21.

for example, or in the countries of North Africa and else-where in Europe. Today's ghettos (like those of yesterday) are perceived as dangerous, economically insecure places, marked by a high rate of immigration, and yet with a cosmopolitan potential for the opportunity to offer different populations to meet and live together.

One of the first to accept and popularize the word "ghetto" as a place name was Louis Wirth, one of the founding fathers of urban sociology in 1925; he did not, however, limit its use only to the Jewish question.[8]

THE FIRST TRANSFORMATIONS

The Ghetto Novo, defined as "spacious" by the Venetian government, was considered "insufficient" by Anselmo, so much so that during the spring and summer of 1516 many Jews left Venice. After 1521, it was above all the Serenissima's tax files that not only attested to the application of the decree, but also to the early transformation of the area, proof that the banker's evaluation was justified.[9] In statements to the Dieci Savi alle Decime in fact, the owners speak of "additions" made by the Jews themselves. Some comparisons between the two tax inquiries conducted respectively in 1514 and in 1521—just before and shortly after the establishment of the Jewish enclosure—clearly show a rapid internal process of fragmentation in undersized apartments, often very small. Even the ground floors had become "little houses." Some (the schoolmaster Simon, an employee at Anselmo's pawnshop, two women who sewed "caps", a widow, and a

---

8. See Epilogue, 147–48.

9. Sanudo, *Diarii*, Vol. 22, col. 86, 20 March 1516; cols. 108–109, 5 April 1516; ASV, *Compilazione Leggi*, b. 189, *Savi alle Decime*, Redecima 1514, b. 44, no. 76; 17 September 1521, no. 77 ("condition" by Da Bruolo).

butcher) went to live in modest accommodations, perhaps in makeshift shacks, either in the attic, or "below", paying however high rents. At the same time, a doctor, an innkeeper, and some *strazzaroli*—ragmen—who had shops in the Rialto until a year earlier, probably could have benefited from more comfortable homes, or at least located "above".

The task of assigning places for housing and work was entrusted to the Ufficio al Cattaver and its technicians.[10]

In the early days, only one tavern was authorized to accommodate Jews passing through. Synagogues, at least officially, still were banned. The lawn of the ancient island with the three wells (their coat of arms can still be seen on one) remained the property of the Da Brolo family, who stipulated the leases for water disposal—with an *acquarolo* who carried water in buckets to the inhabitants of the surrounding buildings and later (from 1605) with the Talmud Torah Confraternity—and even defined places in the campo where meat could be butchered.

Some social divisions were present. A comparison of the financial situation of Giacomo Da Brolo (who happened to be the principal owner of property in the area) in 1514 and that of his son Giovanni seven years later shows that the increase in income derived from ghetto houses was much higher than the 30% expected as a result of the Senate decree. Another 30% increase was due to the number of accommodations created from the interior divisions made to accommodate a much higher number of people than existing homes were able to contain. In short, renting to Jews had proved very profitable, as proven by the testimony of the owners who succeeded Da Brolo in the second half of the century. They certified that the houses were in disrepair, but profitable: "should the *hebrei* leave Venice we would get very little, though the sites are

10. ASV, *Collegio,* Notatorio, 31 January 1537 (1536 m.v.), Reg. 23, fols. 87v–88r and v.

simple and of little importance, and reduced so that Christians would need to spend a lot of money [to live there]."[11]

As early as 1519 there were reports of elevations: Christians owners communicated to the Signoria that they built an attic to hold the collateral of loans made by the banker Anselmo. Subsequent renovations, declared to the Office of the Dieci Savi alle Decime, indicated that the number of property units had multiplied rapidly and was still being recorded in the fifteen years between 1522 and 1537.[12] There certainly great crowding, with the building not only carried out by the owners, but also to a large extent by the tenants. The latter gradually began to take possession of the dwellings to make a series of "improvements" (as they are called in documents) at their own expense, to increase living space.

NEW DISTRICT, NEW LIFE

What needed to be respected *in primis* and by all was the supply of kosher food and also, on certain days, access to the Rialto market.[13]

By the early decades of the sixteenth century, along with the homes, there were butchers, a tavern, and a bakery producing bread in the ghetto; the cheese shops of San Girolamo, almost certainly outside the boundaries and patronized mostly by Christians customers, also sold cheese guaranteed kosher.

The neighborhood was completely organized by the second half of the century. Among the 199 units (homes, shops and

---

11. Quoted in Concina, *Venezia,* 44.

12. This processi s pefectly described by Ennio Concina (ibidem) with precise references to archival documents and to the declarations of the owners Massimo Valier (1566) and Bertuzzi (1585) :

13. Benjamin Ravid, "Kosher Bread in Baroque Venice," *Italia* Jerusalem, Vol. 6, nos. 1-2 (1987): 20–29; ASV, *Notarile, Atti,* Andrea Calzavara ,b. 2993, 24 April 1664.

warehouses) declared by fifty-five owners, the 1582 tax survey found twenty-seven shops in Ghetto Nuovo and Ghetto Vecchio: the pawnshops were excluded from this assessment. They included artisan workshops, even for officially banned but in fact practiced trades (such as the *sartor*, tailor), food shops and *strazzerie* (second hand shops on upper floors, and even outside the boundaries). The shops were similar, open towards the square or the streets with small rooms, paved in Treviso cotto tiles, a window with iron bars, a bare stone bench and wall units (like the Rialto shops) with cabinets and wooden shelves.[14]

The Guardian's House became a real office overlooking the field, with an atrium and adjacent warehouse.[15] For daily water supply four public wells (three in the Ghetto Nuovo and one in the Ghetto Vecchio) were used and the water carriers sold it by the pail, but by then there were also a good number of private wells inside the buildings.[16]

In short, the Jews quickly organized their daily lives. We know that between 1541 and 1590 Rabbi Cain Baruch worked with determination for the safety and maintenance of the houses, paving of roads, availability of some services (for instance a wine store, a greengrocer, and new butcher stands), and to ensure his people greater freedom of movement and simplified access to designated places (sea customs, taxes in the Rialto market).[17]

Equally complex were decisions regarding business activities: some, as we shall see, were allowed to work in Chris-

---

14. ASV, *Notarile*, Atti, 11 July 1582. b. 8869, fols. 104–105v; *Notarile*, Atti, 25 February 1607, b. 1117/1227.

15. ASV, *Savi alle Decime*, 4 June 1546, Reg. 1238, fol. 100v, *Senato Terra*, 31 January 1597 (m.v. 1596), Reg. 66, fols. 165v–172v; *Savi alle Decime* 1582, bb. 161, Castello, 858; 162, Cannaregio 323, 146; 163, Cannaregio, 586; 164, Cannaregio, 1241; 171, DD, 1178, 834; 169, DD, 84.

16. ASV, *Inquisitori agli Ebrei*, 17 September 1638, b. 25, fol. 466.

17. ASV, *Inquisitori agli Ebrei*, 14 March 1590, b. 19, fols. 371r–374v.

tian-owned printing shops or perform with their music and dance companies in the homes of Venetian aristocrats. Others asked and were allowed to live and practice their crafts, such as production of what was once called corrosive sublimate, dangerous enough to require production in previously occupied warehouses, outside the ghetto boundary.[18] More simply, some needed comfortable premises for unloading imported goods in city areas such as the Giudecca, more suitable for storage and industrial production.

Daily life was enriched by shops for basic goods and workplaces. There was a bakery selling leavened and unleavened bread in Ghetto Nuovo and one in Ghetto Vecchio; there were numerous shops of fruit and vegetables, wine, meat, cheese, pasta, and wax candles. There was a barber, a hatter, a mender, a woman educating Jewish girls, a tailor, a bookseller (probably with an attached print and bookbinding shop); a workshop making products for alchemy. And there was an inn for foreign Jews as well as a carver, a lumber warehouse, another for tiles, and storage space for coffins. [19]

PRECARIOUS HOUSING

The buildings facing canals were largely "remanufactured" by the tenants without changing the urban setting: they increased the number of floors and the living area with ledges,

18. ASV, *Ufficiali al Cattaver*, 13 June 1586, b. 242, Reg. 3, fols. 53v–54r; 23 November 1590, b. 243, Reg, 3, fol. 190v, 9 September 1593, b. 244, Reg. 5, fol. 101 v.; 18 February 1595, (m.v. 1594), b. 244, Reg. 5, fol. 137v; 21 October 1631, b. 242, fol. 155; *Compilazione leggi*, 16 May 1655, b. 189, fol. 219; *Senato Terra*, 13 June 1650.

19. ASV, *Savi alle decime*, 1661, b. 426, *Condizion aggiunte* 1589, 2, b. 181, no. 3416, registered on 18 March 1598; *Procuratori di San Marco de ultra*, 10 February 1574 (m. v. 1573), b. 55, fasc. 4, doc. 11, fols. unnumbered; *Notarile,* Atti, Andrea Calzavara, 29 February 1656 (m.v. 1655), b. 2970, fol. 981r.

balconies and *altanelle* (a typical terrace on the roof of venetian buildings, sometimes jutting out over the canal) of
varying size, but also the internal divisions and openings to
the outside. Permits, authorizations, reminders of the terms
of the last charter, as well as punishments and denials, were
frequent.

The original buildings were subdivided in various ways,
and grew in height by increasing the number of floors to
eight or nine, a highly unusual method for a city with sandy
soil notoriously devoid of great resistance. To lighten the
constructions, the walls (not only the partitions, but also the
loadbearing walls) were often very thin, and the distance between the floors, that is, within between floor and ceiling,
was reduced to a acceptable minimum (two or a maximum
2.20 meters).

As unreliable as the census data of these historical periods
are, some figures show us a rapid growth in the population.

The level of promiscuity and hygiene was often unaccept-
able. Small apartments could house "eight or ten and sometimes as many more people as could stay in one constricted
space with a great stench". In addition the Jews, driven by
"insatiable appetites" rented their fellows *"loghetti"*, rooms
without fireplaces, or latrines, with dangerous consequences for hygiene, as confirmed by continuous inspections and
resolutions regarding sanitation in the area.[20] Curious and
significant in this regard is the project for a *scoazera* (an area
for garbage disposal) to be realized in the campo of Ghetto
Nuovo, presented in 1609 by an expert from Belluno, Iseppo
Paolini. He proposed building four large bins or a quantity
of holes in the pavement of the campo as a method of waste

20. Daniele Beltrami, *Storia della popolazione di Venezia dal XVI secolo
alla caduta della Repubblica*, Venice: Milani 1954, 43; ASV, *Provveditori
alla Sanità*, 18 April 1554, C. 1, b. 2, fol. 76v; *Inquisitori agli Ebrei*, n. d.
(but 1600–1605), b. 19, fols. 475–476; 7 August 1604, b. 26, fol. 428.

collection, knowing that neighborhood overcrowding was dangerous for urban living.[21]

There were also infrastructures for lighting and cleaning of roads and wells, a ferry service, periodic dredging of the canals, as well as the water supply for "unhappy people" who did not have their own private wells.

In 1632, even the wooden bridges were declared unsafe, and the estimates required of surveyors and carpenters spoke of a complete makeover.[22]

---

21. ASV, *Secreta, Materie miste e notabili*, b.131, drawing by Iseppo Paolini, 1609.

22. ASV, *Ufficiali al Cattaver*, 6 November 1632, 147 F., b. 242, fol. 254v.

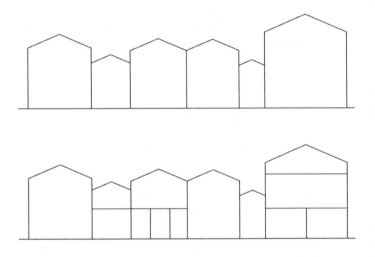

Diagram of the process of densification and internal fragmentation of the buildings in the Ghetto Nuovo, based on the statements made to the Dieci Savi alle Decime in 1514, so just before the establishment of the ghetto, and 1521, five years afterwards.

(Graphics by Alessandra Ferrighi based on theories by Ennio Concina)

3

THE GHETTO EXPANDS

The space available was therefore even considered "constricted" in the early decades of the ghetto's existence. When the Collegio decreed the extension, it instructed the Cinque Savi alla Mercanzia to inspect Cannaregio and examine the area adjacent to the campo. This was done partly with a view to increasing the initial space, now definitely overpopulated, but also to accommodate the new arrivals, the Levantine. Inquisitors reported goods from Romania going to the Jews, who later referred to the authorization obtained from the Senate: trade with the Turks in Constantinople was concentrated in the hands of the Levantines—they said—insisting on "usefulness" of their presence for the Serenissima.

In 1541 however, the Cinque Savi alla Mercanzia identified an almost empty strip of land between the Agudi and Cannaregio canals, with a few vegetable gardens, orchards and old wood board houses, where a wall of adequate height and with a single entrance could be erected outside. The passageway between the two ghettos, communicating but separated, would be located along the Agudi bridge.[1] The characteristics of the area—relatively empty and contiguous to a restricted part of the city, and, especially, concentrated largely in the hands of a single owner (the Minotto family), which would be guaranteed immediate revaluation—made negotiations easier.

---

1. ASV, *Collegio* Notatorio, 8 July 1541, Reg. 24, fol. 118r; 20 luglio 1541, Reg. 24, fol. 120r; *Inquisitori agli Ebrei*, 2 giugno 1541, b. 19, fol. 121 (also in *Senato* same); *Savi alla Mercanzia*, II series, 5 June 1541, b. 62; 16 July 1549, (in *Pregadi* with reference to the decision of 5 June 1547), b. 62; 20 June date 1551, b. 63; *Ufficiali al Cattaver*, 15 December 1609 (in *Pregadi*), b. 2, fols. 13 r.–14 r.

No trade of any kind was allowed in Ghetto Nuovo and new houses for Jews from different countries also had the advantage of ensuring a clearer separation between ethnic groups.

A NEW PLACE OF REFUGE: THE GHETTO VECCHIO

It was soon clear that this was not only a question of increasing living space; the expansion also affected the business areas. After the renewal of the charter in 1558, rag selling was explicitly permitted in the Ghetto Nuovo, and three pawnshops were allowed (but only on the ground floor, to facilitate business dealings). Instead, however, the new inhabitants of Ghetto Vecchio were required to pay additional rent to Christian landlords, taxed and required to apply to the Cinque Savi alla Mercanzia for all permits related to their stay, including the use and distribution of accommodations, taverns and shops.

In point of fact, "no business establishments" were allowed in the Ghetto Nuovo, and the new homes for Jews from different countries also had the advantage of ensuring a clearer separation between ethnic groups.

Even before Collegio instructed the Cinque Savi alla Mercanzia to accommodate the new wave of immigrants—the Levantine Jews—in the Ghetto Vecchio,[2] Abram Luzzatto and his children procured a number of lodgings in the area adjacent to the existing ghetto.[3]

The Ghetto Nuovo, though more densely populated, retained its original form and at the same time became the center for the distribution of services and the site of community identity. The Ghetto Vecchio, however, accentuated its nature as a non-centripetal space arranged along a path functionally

2. ASV, *Collegio,* Notatorio, 8 July 1541, Reg. 24, fol. 118r.

3. ASV, *Procuratori di San Marco de Ultra*, Commissaria da Brolo, 20 March 1537 (m.v 1536)., b. 57, fasc. 24; later: *Savi alle Decime*, Redecima 1582, b. 164, cond. 805.

projected outward, towards the waterways and pedestrian passageway of Cannaregio. It was also distinct from the point of
view of the area's growing density. Originally run down and
full of unconstructed areas (gardens, yards, courtyards), for
over a century some cultivated areas and gardens remained, as
the *proto alle acque* (Surveyor of Waters) Bernardino Zendrini
certified in 1680 when the waters of the Cannaregio canal were
dredged.[4] The surface was then gradually filled, accentuating
the contrast between the narrowness of some streets and the
relative monumentality of the two synagogues—the Spanish
(or Ponentine) and Levantine.

1589: A TURNING POINT

The Senato Mare resolution was passed in 1589 to encourage
the increase in commercial traffic. It reiterated the importance of "opening the way" for those wishing to reach Venice,
and while the residence of the Jews was subject to periodic
renewal, it was no longer in question. The Levantine Jews
from the Ottoman Empire and the western Jews from Spain
and Portugal were officially admitted with their families and
encouraged to put down roots in the city. They were allowed
to practice freely "using and performing their rituals, pre-
cepts, and ceremonies, keeping up synagogues, according
to their custom, and safe from being] molested." They had
the option of "traveling by sea, buying, selling and trading."
They could import any goods to Venice by paying a duty like
everyone else.[5] This was a breakthrough of major importance
in relations between the Serenissima and the Jewish minority.

---

4. Bernardino Zendrini, *Memorie storiche dello stato antico e moderno
delle lagune di Venezia*, Venice: 1726, BMC, Ms P. D., 240, tome 1, Libro VIII, fol. 1037.

5. ASV, *Senato Mare*, 27 July 1589, Reg. 50, fols. 58v–60r; 6 October
1598, Reg. 68, fols. 94r–95v.

In the campo of Ghetto Nuovo, the rhythms of daily life were punctuated by daylight, the opening and closing of the doors of the pawnshops and rag sellers, while the large trapezoid square hosted deals, meetings, study, and ceremonies. Near the Cannaregio canal, however, the pulse was the long and discontinuous pace of international trade and immigration from far away.

These measures encouraged Marranos from other Italian cities to be circumcised, then to go to Constantinople and finally return to Venice as Levantine Jews. The capital of the Serenissima had always been a "frontier" where conversions, switching from one religion to another, were routinely practiced. With all of that even the changing identity of Marranos became "normal".[6]

Even if the Jews never became "subjects" with full rights, from then on, they enjoyed relative equality, especially the Levantine and western Jews, not only regarding payment of duties on imports, but also in the much more meaningful ease of sailing the seas and access to trade bases in the Mediterranean.

At the time of turning point, in 1589, the population of the Ghettos Nuovo and Vecchio amounted to 1,600 people; between the end of that century and the beginning of the next it reached 1642, with growth higher than the rest of the city. This figure was further increased by the presence of the Marranos in the city, whom the Doge Leonardo Donato defended before the Apostolic Nuncio, saying that they should be regarded as Jews, and therefore could not be judged by the Holy Office.[7] After the annexation of the Ghetto Nuovissimo in 1633, there were 2414 people (there were 454 victims of the plague in the area). In 1654, with a further increase of 50 percent, the population reached 4870, i.e. 3 percent of the to-

6. Riccardo Calimani, *Il ghetto di Venezia*, Milan: Rusconi 1985, 97–111, 112–37 ; Giuseppina Minchella, *Frontiere aperte. Musulani, ebrei, cristiani*, Rome: Viella 2014, 31–34.

7. Gaetano Cozzi, s.v. "Leonardo Donà," in *Dizionario Biografico degli Italiani*, Vol. 40, Rome: Istituto dell'Enciclopedia Italiana 1991.

tal population of the center of Venice, with a density between two and four times higher than the rest of the urban context.[8]

The effects of the plague of 1630, dramatic for the entire city, were even more profound in an area where overcrowding facilitated the spread of the epidemic: for that reason, in 1661, a number of buildings were declared "empty." But the process of stratification soon resumed, and towards the end of the century even the number of courtyards and open spaces appeared diminished, changing the way land was occupied. [9]

FRONTIERS BETWEEN THE COMMUNITIES

If it is fair to say that all Jews were engaged in commerce, in fact they worked differently. For this reason, they enjoyed dissimilar privileges and paid duties in variable percentages. They also used the space assigned them differently, creating a personal relationship with the city and use of its physical spaces.

The administrative, economic and even legal role of Jewish merchants, Greek-speaking or of Byzantine origin, had become crucial in relations between the commercial base of the Mediterranean and the Ottoman Empire, of which Venice was one of the main centers. Both the structure of the market with the Levant and the mindset of the Venetian nobility, only too happy to delegate trade with Eastern Europe to the Jews, were changing. The latter had the task of ensuring a continuous flow of money to the capital, so that they were often settled in the Adriatic, with the consent and complicity of the Republic. But they didn't always live in areas isolated by walls, though

8. Gino Luzzatto, "Sulla condizione degli Ebrei veneziani nel secolo XVIII," *Rassegna Mensile d'Israel* 16 (1950): 161; Aldo Contento, "Il censimento della popolazione della Repubblica Veneta," *Nuovo Archivio Veneto* 19 (1900): 5–42, 179–240, 20: 5–96; L. A. Schiavi, "Gli ebrei di Venezia e nelle sue colonie", *Nuova Antologia*, ser. 3, 47 (1893): 491–92.

9. ASV, *Savi alle Decime*, 1661, bb. 425 e 426; Sanudo, *Diarii*, Vol. 52, October 28, 1529.

sometimes these were erected because of correspondence with dangerous, smelly or noisy jobs (such as dye works). Different attitudes and different degrees of tension between groups more or less protected by the Dominante (another name for the Republic of Venice) were therefore encountered.[10]

However, at the end of the sixteenth century, the Senate insisted that the Germans and Italians, Levantine "wayfarers" and "inhabitants", and western and Spanish Jews had equal value for the public administration since they were all merchants in the territory of the state.[11] This was reaffirmed by the Cinque Savi alla Mercanzia, the magistrates with whom, despite controversy and difficulty of relationships, the Cattaver shared tasks. The former were responsible for the Levant and western Jews as regarded housing, the burial of the dead, mercantile conflicts, and the payment of duties; the latter were final judges for the German and Italian Jews. The two courts had different areas of jurisdiction: one towards Cannaregio Canal and San Girolamo for the other. They also had to find ways of attracting and forcing those German Jews—who, "for lack of homes", had over the years invaded the land of others—to live in the first ghetto.

In short, management of the area and buildings was difficult and full of challenges, as was the opening and location of shops. Attempts to establish boundaries, preserve rights, and add new clauses, and privileges of partial immunity were constant, but—as often happened in the long history of the Venetian Republic—disputes arose between organs with partially overlapping

10. Bernhard Blumenkranz, "Les Juifs dans le commerce maritime de Venise 1592-1609," *Revue des Etudes Juives,* ser. 3, 2 (1961): 143–151; Arieh Shmuelevitz, *The Jews of the Ottoman Empire in the late Fifteenth and Sixteenth Centuries,* Leiden: Brill 1984; David Jacoby, "Venetian Jews in the Eastern Mediterranean," and Bernard Dov Cooperman, "Venetian Policy Towards Levantine Jews," in Gaetano Cozzi, (ed.), *Gli Ebrei e Venezia*, Milan: Edizioni di Comunità 1987, 29–58 and 65–84.

11. ASV, *Savi alla Mercanzia,* II ser., 27 July 1589, (in *Pregadi*), b. 62, 6 October 1598 (in *Pregadi*), fasc. 168.

responsibilities (of the *Ufficiali alle Razon Vecchie, Dieci Savi alle Decime, Savi ed Esecutori alle Acque, Giudici del Piovego, Giudici del Proprio*).[12] Moreover, the Jews possessed their own governing body, independent of the judiciary of the Republic: an assembly of heads of families and a supranational council of deputies were in charge of internal affairs and held individual community offices. In particular, representatives were in charge of taxation and distribution of contributions and debts, preventing corruption and the administration of justice. In fact, they constituted an additional means of organizing public life and managing the area's urban services (night security, lighting of public spaces and synagogues, water supply, street cleaning, sanitary control of meat).[13]

New food shops were opened in different Jewish communities: an oil "and other common foods" shop was set up in 1617. The route from home to shops was reduced to a minimum: The Ghetto Vecchio had different butcher, greengrocer, and wine shops from those of the neighboring Ghetto Nuovo. Delivery of bread, wine, meat, fruits and vegetables to the property of the noble Querini family had to operate "without prejudice", i.e. without competition between close, but different Jewish groups.[14]

In fact, in the new expanded area, relations with the city were quite different: for the Republic, newcomers meant boosting trade with the markets of the East and representing Venice in the Dominion's sea ports.[15] Requests from the count and

---

12. ASV, *Ufficiali al Cattaver*, 15 December 1609 (in *Pregadi*), b. 2, fols. 13r–14r; *Senato Terra*, 10 July 1636, Reg. 114, fols. 168r–171r.

13. Umberto Fortis, *Il ghetto in laguna*, Venice: Storti 1967, table on page 80.

14. The identification of shops and services in the areas of the three ghettos has been carried out comparing the information from 1661, 1713, and 1740; see Donatella Calabi, "Il ghetto e la città, 1541–1866," in Ennio Concina, Donatella Calabi, Ugo Camerino, (eds.), *La città degli Ebrei. Il ghetto di Venezia, architettura e urbanistica*, Venice: Albrizzi 1991, 296–97, notes 80–81.

15. ASV, *Savi alla Mercanzia*, 20 June 1590, II ser., b. 63, fasc. 108, fol. 7.

captain of Split, the Count of Trogir, from the mayor of Klis, and from Turkish ministers to activate the 'Scala' (a kind of customhouse) in Split and improve conditions of the Jews in Venice and in Dalmatia, thus appear very significant.

Indeed, in 1598 at the time of a routine renewal of the charter for the Levantine and western merchants, a certain Daniel Rodriguez submitted a petition (in a sense from a position of strength). Often called Rodriga in Venetian, Rodriquez was an enterprising Spanish Jew, full of initiative, who—after decades of moving from one plaza of the Mediterranean to another—set himself up in one of the houses belonging to Minotto in Ghetto Vecchio. Considered the commendable inventor of the customhouse of Split, he was sent to Dalmatia at state expense to press for completion of the project proposed and undertaken a few years before, i.e. refurbish the port and the construction of a quarantine hospital and customhouse "for the convenience and use" of the Signoria, in view of relations with the Ottoman empire. Daniel Rodriguez introduced a real free port and became the Republic's agent, entrusted with great responsibility.[16]

THE LAST EXPANSION: GHETTO NUOVISSIMO

At the beginning of the seventeenth century, the Jewish population was about 3,000, despite the demographic decline caused by one of the most serious plague epidemics in Venetian history. Although there had been pressure for additional space for the Jews for over thirty years, a new area, the Ghetto Nuovissimo, destined to host another wave of immigration, was only then established.

In 1633 the Cinque Savi alla Mercanzia were charged by the

16. ASV, *Savi alle decime*, 1582, b. 160, Castello / 782, declaration by Zuane Minotto, q. Bernardo; *Ufficiali al Cattaver*, 2 October 1604, b. 246, fol. 3v; *Savi alla Mercanzia*, II ser., 17 May 1604, b. 62; Benjamin Ravid, "The First Charter of the Jewish Merchants of Venice 1589," *Association for the Jewish Studies Review* I (1976): 187–222.

Senate to review the sites, conduct a survey, deal with the owner of the area behind Ca' Zanoli (or Zanelli), build a bridge of communication and suggest the form of twenty new homes to keep "locked and embedded" in the ghetto for twenty "families of newcomers".[17] To this purpose, measurements were taken of the thirty-two homes belonging to Zanelli "of condition grandeur and respectable nobility", behind which were two lines of houses on one floor and an attic, with a spacious adjacent square that allowed for construction of a new bridge to the Ghetto Nuovo. The project and enlargement were at the expense of the Jews, who were also to ensure its maintenance. The premises of the existing butcher had to be avoided, or perhaps the costs of moving the stands were covered, giving Marco Da Brolo, son of Bernardo, a fee of 500 ducats to grant a passageway (a sottoportico) within his buildings. Two shops, one toward the campo and the other overlooking the canal, were sacrificed.[18]

Once pedestrian access over the river was built, and after the *proto al sale* (Surveyor of Salt) Bettinelli had verified the quality of the work, the leaders of the Levantine and western Jews were permitted to urge the arrival of persons "of good report," offering them "large and spacious" homes. In order to cope with the excessive density of the neighboring area, no internal transfers—considered several times in previous decades—were planned. However, the aim was to attract more foreigners to Venice to benefit the city economy. To this end, and to ensure stability and security, passage between the ghettos

17. Gino Luzzatto, "Sulla condizione degli Ebrei veneziani nel secolo XVIII," *La Rassegna Mensile d'Israel* 16 (1950): 161; the number may be overestimated if we consider the data supplied in Daniele Beltrami, *Storia della popolazione di Venezia dal XVI secolo alla caduta della Repubblica*, Venice: Milani 1954, 43; ASV, *Senato Terra*, 16 September 1632, fol. 347; 3 March 1633, Reg. 109, fols. 6v–7r and v.

18. ASV, *Procuratori de San Marco de ultra*, 22 September, 6 October, 10 November 1633, b. 57, fols. unnumbered.

was completely banned for at least three years. [19] Nonetheless, even in this case, the increase in the population and physical stratification followed a more accelerated and confused pace than expected. Moreover, even before the construction of the bridge, the houses and the small campo belonging to Commissar Malipiero had been granted to Jews. Conversely, there was a relative decrease in population density per hectare in the Ghetto Vecchio after the building Ghetto Nuovissimo which instead grew quickly enough: contrary to the rules, there had been a partial movement of people between contiguous areas. [20]

Thirty years later, however, the number of houses of the Ghetto Nuovissimo rose from twenty to twenty-seven; by 1740 they had doubled and were equipped with amenities. In 1661, nineteen were provided with a well and three with an altana or covered terrace. There were twenty warehouses, more or less related to the residence and distinct from those places in the attic spaces. In the second half of the eighteenth century in the area we find a confraternity devoted to education with premises for a school, a storeroom for firefighting material, one to keep pails and tubs, and a carpentry shop. Ultimately, it was a small group of houses quite different from each other. The rent, which varied between that for housing leased "for the love of God" and other premises rented for 100 ducats, was proof of how the ghetto became a rapidly changing periphery, though containing large buildings and valuable architecture. [21]

Emblematic of this wave of immigration and the role that Ghetto Nuovissimo and more generally the lagoon city quickly assumed, is the case of ship owner Isaac Treves. He reached Venice from Constantinople—where his father Mandolin Emanuel had settled around the middle of the seventeenth century,

19. ASV, *Senato Terra*, 3 March 1633, Reg. 109, fols. 6v–7r and v.

20. Beltrami, *Storia della popolazione di Venezia*, 30.

21. ASV, *Savi alle Decime*, 1661, bb. 426, 1126.

opening a major firm of mercantile traffic with the help of his brother-in-law Israel Conegliano (powerful secretary of the bailiff of the Venetian Republic at the Sublime Porte, despite the unmistakably Jewish name). In 1724, Isaac Treves with a certain Brown from London founded a commercial enterprise that also moved in the credit sector. Creator and commissioner of "Venetian Baltic Company for Russia, Sweden and Denmark," Isaac won control of traffic to Northern Europe and in the direction towards Lisbon. From there he pushed further towards the Americas, maintaining the exclusive of those routes for over a century.

The family, whose members showed a great musical culture and sensitivity, a keen interest in books, porcelain and textiles from the imperial court of Petersburg, owned several warehouses in the city—on the Giudecca and near the ghetto—for the storage of coffee, which they imported in large quantities. In 1780 they also became owners of eight rooms to store the goods inside the Ghetto Nuovissimo.

Their residence inside the expanded area consisted of two large houses, a combined double building containing four apartments overlooking the San Girolamo Canal at the Ormesini bridge with ground access from the back street. From here, there was also passage to the nearby palace of the Vivante family (from Corfu), with whom the Treves were also related by marriage. In the late eighteenth century, both families—no longer subject to restrictions of movement—obtained permission to build a water gate to unload their wares, open directly to the outside of the boundary like the most important mansions in the lagoon.[22]

At the end of the seventeenth century, all of the three ghettos became therefore mainly residential urban neighborhoods, but equipped, albeit differently, with special privileges for each, very densely inhabited. In this it was not altogether dissimilar

22. Martina Massaro, *Giacomo Treves de Bonfili, collezionista e mecenate (1788-1885)*, Ph.D. thesis. Venice 2013-2014, 8–22.

from other Italian ghettos founded in the meantime (in Rome, Florence, Siena, Verona, Ferrara, and Modena).

In short, during the seventeenth century, that space that Francesco Sansovino defined as the "small town" of the Jews varied immensely: the three nations (German, Levantine and Spanish) lived together in distinct and often conflicting, bordering areas, variously adapting to street and building patterns. Some processes of community organization had also begun. Not only did that not deny the differences, but rather reaffirmed them, since the varying use of space and time depended on the inhabitants' origin.

There were also ongoing difficulties in relations between the Ufficiali al Cattaver and the Cinque Savi alla Mercanzia, which sometimes negotiated with each other regarding "adjustments" in occupation of space by people who should be confined to other parts of the neighborhood. Other times they were forced to require Christian landlords to make "improvements" or throw a tenant out in favor of a needier candidate.

These episodes highlighted the challenges involved in keeping the various communities and families with diverse financial resources separate, goals desired and pursued by the Venetian magistrates to guarantee social peace, but difficult to achieve due to the lack of available space. These social and economic provisions were part of a precise urban strategy and at the base of different and detailed forms of planned segregation, entailing however a high risk of concentration and internal divisions.

A SPECIAL LEGAL SYSTEM

During the fifteenth century and not only in Venice, Jews were banned from buying or having custody of real estate, funds, leases or lands.[23] In the lagoon in 1531, following requests

---

23. ASV, *Compilazione Leggi*, 16 February 1423, 26 September 1423, 30 December 1424, b. 188; see, s.v. "hasakah," in *The Jewish Encyclopedia*, Vol. 6, New York-London: Funk and Wagnalls, 1904; s.v. "Jew-

submitted to the Signoria by Salamon Dal Banco (the pawn-shop owner) and other "comrades," relating to construction carried out in the ghetto, the Collegio admitted the scale of the work done by residents in homes and shops, also decreeing that it was not "suitable" that the burdens assumed could turn into "convenience for others." Without denying the ban on full acquisition, the consequences of this stance proved crucial: users could dispose of these assets at will and sell them as they wished, provided that the owners were guaranteed due rent. In actual fact, it was a form of 'possession' of buildings of the ghetto, thus guaranteed to the Jews, with the implicit right to modify the structure: increasing volume, intervening in the functional distribution, dividing interior spaces, as well as making bequests or a donation, and even subletting. All this corresponded to the Jewish legal formula of jus *Hasakah* (also defined according to the Latin-Spanish expression as *gazaga* or in the Venetian version, *casacà*, or *casacod*) indicating the possibility for people to earn income from the possession acquired as well as from "improvements" made. It was a privilege, only encoded in the seventeenth century by Pope Clement VII, that allowed the tenant to lease as long as he regularly paid the rent (plus one third), with the Community as guarantor of prompt payment. This right was enjoyed by Jews in Venice as well as in Rome, Ancona and Modena.

This decision may be in effect interpreted as a form of 'integration' of the Jewish minority, a phenomenon that became apparent in the city within seventy years. In 1583, in fact, the Rialto office of the Dieci Savi alle Decime, in charge of collection of property taxes for the entire city, decided that the Jews—as with all owners of houses, shops, and warehouses—should de-

---

ish quarter," in *Encyclopaedia Judaica*, Vol.7, Jerusalem: Keter 1971; Marco Ferro, *Dizionario del diritto comune e veneto*, Volume 5, Venice: Modesto Fenzo 1779, 4; Giuseppe Boerio, s.v. "casacà," in *Dizionario del dialetto veneziano*, Venice: Giovanni Cecchini 1856.

clare any earnings arising from their properties.[24] Some went to the offices right away, without using the word casacà but instead referring to the practice reserved for Christian citizens, and made the declaration; others actually went spontaneously even before the decision was formalized, and those in charge of the office imposed the tithe. Furthermore, the archives also document the passage of "possession" or "improvements" of the houses of the ghetto from one individual to another in the second half of the sixteenth century. Essentially the jus Hasakah was a transferable right that could be given by way of family inheritance, dowry, donation, purchase or sale. Ever since then even notaries were found to record a series of transactions of portions of building "improvements" between patricians or Christian citizens and Jewish tenants with acts that explicitly evoke sales of casacà against an exchange of money.[25]

With time, conflicts were inevitable: between 1636 and 1641 Marco Da Brolo, a descendant of the original owner, complained for example to the Procuratori di San Marco that he received an inadequate income for his forty-six houses, which the Jewish tenants were "trading". Some properties were still in their original state, but were sublet at a higher price than actually owed, while in others minimal renovations had been made with great benefit for both tenants and landlords; the same was true for a butcher shop.[26] Da Brolo found it necessary

---

24. ASV, *Savi alle Decime, Sommario et pratica generale delle leggi, terminationi et ordeni dell'Exc. mo Senato, Maggior Consiglio et officio degli Illustrissimi Signori X Savi sopra le Decime fatto da Gerolamo Borella*, b. 8, fols. 148, 167; Capitolare II, 7 November 1583, b. 2, 1463-1685, fol. 154r.

25. Ennio Concina, *Venezia nell'età moderna*, in *La città degli Ebrei*, Venice: Marsilio 1989, 88n12; Carla Boccato, "Istituzione del ghetto veneziano: il diritto di locazione perpetua o 'jus gazaga' ed i banchi di pegno," *Giornale economico della Camera di Commercio, industria, artigianato e agricoltura di Venezia* no. 3 (May-June 1971): 340.

26. ASV, *Procuratori di San Marco de Ultra*, Commissaria da Brolo, 28 April 1637, b. 56, fasc. 11-12, fol. 3.

to reiterate that the Jews did not have "ownership" of those houses; if they did not want to live in them, the tenants should return them to him. He stated that he was willing to pay for any improvements, and that prices should take their conditions into account. Then again, there were those elsewhere who benefited from these improvements, varying the rent each time, such as Camilla Minotto in the area bordering the Ghetto Vecchio. Rabbi Simon Luzzatto, however, brought up the substantial investments made by his coreligionists and stressed the similarities between the terms used in Venetian and in Jewish law.

It is quite understandable that there was malcontent over ownership of buildings, initially of only one or two floors that later grew in height and therefore in volume, along with the fact that rental mechanisms were partially freed from the surface actually enjoyed. There were numerous petitions, records, appeals to the Doge and the Collegio, until the Senate resolved in 1641 to appoint a commission to settle disputes.

Ultimately, by that time there was a clear difference between buildings still in their original state and others that had been renovated or rebuilt.[27] The casacà had officially become the object of sale, so that the new owner could build "in accordance with the laws and Jewish rituals and the charter" and notaries could note these acts as "more hebreorum" (Jewish customs) or even as perpetual, in clear contradiction with fifteenth-century Venetian law.

During the seventeenth and eighteenth centuries, the word casacà even became synonymous with building. Some documents from notary archives use the term primarily referring to houses in poor condition made of wooden planks, to precarious attic dwellings, or those placed over a pre-existing floor.

---

27. ASV, *Procuratori di San Marco de Ultra*, Commissaria de Brolo, 28 April 1637, b.56, fasc. 10, fol. 14.

Page of a register with the names of people who pawned objects at Banco Rosso and amount of their debts due six months after January 1, 1759. Some claim that the expression "be in the red" to define a situation of financial deficit was derived from the Banco Rosso di Ghetto Nuovo.

(ASV, *Quarantia Criminal*, filza 448, Ebrei, fol. 288r)

4

PERMITTED TRADES

As in the major European commercial centers (Antwerp, Nuremberg, and Amsterdam), the tendency to divide the city into specialized sectors was consistent with an ancient desire, reconfirmed again and again, to welcome people of distant countries who spoke different languages, practiced other religions, and lived their lives according to different habits to the lagoon.

Gradually, other foreign communities specialized in some specific services requiring a diversified division of the urban fabric: the trade of fustian and wool cloth was entrusted to the *Alemanni* (Germans), that of gold to subjects of the Ottoman Empire, silk became the prerogative of the Florentines, and the art of printing and typesetting was in the hands of Armenians.

By tradition, the Jews were mostly bankers and pawnbrokers, as well as traders of second-hand items. Over time, Senate authorization repeatedly reaffirmed these activities as their prevalent urban occupations.

However, between the middle of the sixteenth and the nineteenth centuries, Jewish occupations in Venice, on and off their 'island' changed significantly, impacting relations between the residential area subject to restrictions for a part of the population, and the rest of the city. Trade, as well as linguistic and cultural exchange in the Mediterranean basin, corresponded to a network of relations, for instance with Madrid, as well as trade fairs in Piacenza or Besancon. They were well certified by the strong international character of certain seventeenth century women's wills giving bequests to Jewish confraternities, Venetian welfare institutions such as hospitals, the ghetto poor, or more commonly their families.

Goods, money, credits and jewels that remained outside Venice, like those of Judith, widow of the Spanish Jew Antonio Mendez, were bequeathed to her daughter Rachel, her son Pietro Anriquez, and her nephew Michael, who only lived in Venice for certain periods. The act was signed in the presence of a witness obviously from outside the family, of Polish origin, a wine *travasador* (a bottler).[1]

The socio-economic stratification of the various nations living in the ghetto was conspicuous in the varying sources of livelihood, and the diverse quality of housing. As we have seen, along with pawn broking, other occupations coexisted: the art of medicine and the sale of used goods (the so-called *strazzaria*) alongside humbler home service and minor jobs. There was also a great deal of maritime traffic with large and profitable commerce in the trade hubs Levante, the Near East

But one calling had a special place and symbolized better than all the others the ongoing interchange between nations: printing.

PRINTING AND THE SPREADING OF IDEAS

With the spread of printed books at the end of the fifteenth, and even more in the sixteenth century, cultural exchange intensified. Study of Hebrew was particularly popular in Venice, an emblem of the recovery of the ancient civilization, especially among the nobles who enjoyed easier access to culture and were attracted by the innovations of humanism. Since Jews were forbidden to practice the trade of publishing, they become assistants as advisors, proofreaders, and typesetters, based on their knowledge of Hebrew.

---

1. Carla Boccato, "Aspetti patrimoniali e beneficiari nei testamenti di donne ebree veneziane del Seicento," in *Donne a Venezia, Spazi di libertà e forme di potere (secoli XVI-XVIII)*, conference proceedings (Venice, 8–10 May 2008), Venice: CEISVEN 2012, 7-10 <www.storia divenezia.net/sito/donne/Boccato_Aspetti.pdf>

Hebrew played a leading role: in 1498 Gershom Soncino, a native of Speyer, moved to Venice and met Aldus Manutius, who was printing Poliziano's *Omnia Opera* (Complete Works) with some Hebrew characters. The following year (1499) the language appeared in the pages and woodcuts of *Hypnerto-machia Polphili* (Poliphilo's Strife of Love in a Dream)—particularly in inscriptions placed above the three bronze doors that the book's hero meets on his allegorical journey—and other books published by the famous humanist. A grammar, *Introductio per brevis ad hebraicam linguan* (Brief Introduction to Hebrew), was printed by the same Aldus between 1501 and 1503, almost certainly due to his collaboration with Soncino, whose name, however, does not appear in the publication. Later, Soncino's relations with Manutius broke off abruptly when he moved to Fano, taking with him Francesco Grifo who, in 1496, had designed and produced for Aldo the first Greek italics characters.[2]

After the death of Aldus—who had never obtained written permission to print Hebrew, although he in fact used it[3]—the Christian printshop of Cornelis van Bombergen (a businessman from Antwerp who settled in Venice in 1515) and his son Daniel obtained the exclusive privilege of printing Hebrew books for the following decade from the Collegio. The name of Daniel Bomberg is therefore linked to the first edition of the Babylonian Talmud, printed between 1520 and 1523, as well as the *editio princeps* of the *Biblia Rabinica*, printed in 1516-1517 in association with the Augustinian friar Felice da Prato, an apostate Jew. In 1515, the latter had asked the Senate for

---

2. Giulio Busi, *L'enigma dell'ebraico nel Rinascimento*, Turin: Aragno 2007, 129–44.

3. Avraham Rosenthal, "Daniel Bomberg and his Talmud Editions," in Gaetano Cozzi, (ed.), *Gli Ebrei e Venezia*, Milan: Edizioni di Comunità 1987, 375–416; Simonetta Pelusi, (ed.), *La civiltà del Libro e la stampa a Venezia,* conference proceedings (Venice, Fondazione Cini, 2000), Padua: Il Poligrafo 2000.

permission to print his translations and annotated editions of the Talmud with new, especially created Hebrew characters, making use of four Jewish employees who were therefore allowed to circulate in Venice without the "bereta zala" (yellow cap).[4] These publications in general came in two versions, one for Christian readers interested in Hebrew studies, the other for a Jewish audience. What is certain is that many of the prayer books and some of the biblical content or liturgical manuscripts published by Bomberg (up to 1549) were also ordered by distant Jewish communities—Greece, Aleppo, and Constantinople—in contact with Venice. This is important evidence of the familiar cultural exchange especially in the Mediterranean basin. The use of Jewish labor had proved crucial.

As a merchant, Bomberg remained very attached to his country of origin, and became an essential point of reference for a Venetian nobleman and scholar of great prestige, Domenico Grimani, for whom he was the intermediary of choice for the import of Flemish tapestries and works of art, including the famous painting by Hieronymus Bosch now in the Palace of Santa Maria Formosa. In Antwerp, Bomberg maintained close contacts with the Mendes bank, whose direct channels facilitated delivery to Venice of the assets of Marrano Jews, for this purpose entertaining excellent business relations with the Jews settled in the lagoon. The exchange of goods and knowledge went hand in hand, and the Jewish minority, with their assorted origins and components, were the decisive medium. In moments of tension and persecution, books become symbolic instruments of power. On the model of papal attacks, like in Rome a few copies

---

4. ASV, *Collegio,* Notatorio, 23 April 1515, 27 May 1515, 16 June 1515, Reg. 18, fol. 3v; *Senato Terra,* 15 April 1518, *Consilio dei X,* Comune, Reg. II, fol. 8, *Consiglio dei X,* Notatorio, Reg. II, fols. 154, 278; Giuliano Tamani, *L'attività tipografica a Venezia fra il 1516 e il 1627,* in Umberto Fortis, (ed.), *Venezia ebraica,* Rome: Carocci 1982, 85–97.

of the Talmud were burned in Venice in Piazza San Marco in 1553.[5] The case of the monumental code on Jewish law *Shulhan Arukh*, published for the first time in Venice in 1565 and then in Krakow between 1578 and 1580, with its enormous impact on relations between Ashkenazi and Sephardi culture, is a significant example of the regular migration of Hebrew books from Venice to eastern Europe in those years. Moreover, the publication of biblical commentaries written in Venice which then traveled to Constantinople, Amsterdam and elsewhere in the East, allowed the circulation of Ashkenazi writings in Sephardic libraries, disseminating Italian and Spanish sermons and revitalizing the philosophical tradition of Eastern Europe, ultimately forming a modern, interconnected Jewish culture.[6]

Some years later, when there were numerous Hebrew prayer books, Talmudic compendiums, dictionaries and grammars printed in Venice using Jewish curators, proofreaders and composers, Hebrew also popped up on the Istrian stone facade of the church of San Zulian: two side epigraphs in Greek and Hebrew respectively, smaller than the central Latin, were engraved in cartouches between two pairs of fluted Doric semi-columns flanking the portal (fig. 2). They gave the date of the church (1554) according to Byzantine calculation and the Jewish era of creation.[7] It therefore seems significant that the doctor and Christian philologist, Tommaso Rangone—who settled in Venice in 1532, and cultivated close relations with the aristocracy as an agent of churches and monasteries, and patron of Jacopo Sansovino—wanted to use inscriptions related to the cul-

5. Riccardo Calimani, *Il ghetto di Venezia*, Milan: Rusconi 1985, 88–89.

6. David. B. Ruderman, *Early Modern Jewry: A New Cultural History*, Princeton, NJ: Princeton University Press 2010, 99–102.

7. Nicolò Zorzi, "L'iscrizione trilingue di Tommaso Rangoni," *Quaderni per la Storia dell'Università di Padova* no. 45 (2012): 107–138.

tures of the ancient civilizations (including, by definition, Hebrew) as a celebratory "monument" to confirm his standing as a man of letters.

By then, Bomberg's work had been replaced by that of other Christian nobles of Venetian origin: They included Marco Antonio Giustiniani, whose printshop was located near the Rialto market (1545-1552), and Alvise Bragadin (starting in 1550), as well as smaller printers who partially adopted Bomberg's characters (Giovanni da Gara, the Zanetti brothers, and Giovanni Grifio).

In Venice, biblical and rabbinic literature also played an important role. In these fields, there were talented grammarians (the aforementioned physician Abraham de Balmes and Rabbi Samuel Archivolti, for example), diligent philologists (such as Elijah Levita) and learned theologians (Isac Cardoso, Leon da Modena, and Simon Luzzatto). The humanistic tendencies and attraction to Kabbalistic speculation melded in an atmosphere of cosmopolitan syncretism, where Christian scholars, converted Jews, and orthodox Jews all moved.[8]

We also know that—especially starting in the seventeenth century—private citizens founded circles and academies to spread and extend knowledge of Jewish culture and sacred texts.[9] One of the most significant characters in this sense was Sara Coppio Sullam, who lived in Venice between the end of the sixteenth and the first half of the seventeenth century, and came from a family involved in trade, originally from Mantua. She was a connoisseur of history, philosophy, classical literature, Jewish traditions, blonde and very beautiful, who composed music and verse. The best known of her

8. *Venezia e le sue lagune*, Vol. 1, Venice: Antonelli 1847, 105; Roberto Bonfil, "Cultura e mistica ebraica," in Cozzi, ed., *Gli Ebrei e Venezia*, 478, 481.

9. Cozzi, *Gli Ebrei e Venezia*, 179.

patrons and friends was Leon Modena, who often visited her salon, open to Gentiles as well as Jews.[10]

MONEYLENDING

Instead, in contrast to the rest of Italy, Venice remained one of the few places where the Jewish pawn shops resisted the advance of the *monte di pietà* (the institutionalized money lending charities set up by the Catholic church). The lagoon inhabitants' traditional mistrust towards religious charities, but above all the cooperation between the government and the Jewish community underway since the fourteenth century, distinguished Venice from most cities on the mainland. Another factor was the fact that the Jewish loans, much faster and more versatile, were extremely useful in a major trade center, inevitably linked to the economic fluctuations and political situations in Europe.

Initial bans and subsequent exemptions were related to the crisis of Cambrai and ended up favoring both those who enhanced their own chances of survival by pawning the few goods they owned, and those needing large sums to invest. The sensible choice made by the Consiglio dei Dieci and some prestigious senators such Antonio Grimani in 1523, moved in this direction with the consent of the Doge Andrea Gritti. In a public session, he impressed on his listeners that the Jews had become absolutely "necessary" to the city poor.[11] The operation was much more complex than its words reveal: it acknowledged that loans were a socio-economic balancing factor and a service to the less affluent, as well as directly to the Signoria and wealthy merchants that made up the Republic's backbone.

---

10. Giorgio Busetto, s.v. "Copio Sara," in *Dizionario Biografico degli italiani*, Rome: Vol. 28, Istituto dell'Enciclopedia Italiana, 1983.

11. Simon Luzzatto, *Discorso circa lo stato degl'hebrei et in particolar dimoranti nell'inclita città di Venetia*, Venice: Calleoni 1638, 1.

In fact, even the wealthy citizens and nobles resorted to these services. So, it was a task delegated to foreigners, but regulated by clauses, hours of operation, type of goods, contractual arrangements, and appointed magistrates. The pawnshops were ultimately the public fixture of a great local and international market, a tool for compel Jews to remain in Venice by filtering their physical isolation with mutual benefit.[12]

The aforementioned charter renewal of 1558, authorizing the presence of three pawnbrokers under the control of a scribe ("Red" bank whose name can still be read today beneath the portico in the campo, "Black" bank and "Green" bank), also indicated the need for specific office or a wooden foyer. It stated that the pawnshops be located on the ground floor and that they could have shelters or storage places for the store to deposit the items left in pledge. Rates had to be clearly visible on signboards and translated into the common language (like for taxes owed by those who frequent the stores of the Germans, Persians, and Turks), so that users could easily understand the fees.

Later charter renewals allowed other pawnbrokers to open; there were five in 1565, but the Board of the University of the Jews (i.e. the Jewish Community) presented a list of eleven companies that lent money to the state, most of which located in the lagoon city.[13] The location of the three original banks, subcontracted to private households for a limited period, remained the same around the campo of Ghetto Nuovo, even when those in charge alternated or the first bankers were assigned lending to others. The first was located along the

---

12. ASV, *Senato Terra*, 13 June 1525, Reg. 24, fol. 12; 16 November 1624, Reg. 94, fols. 211v–227r; Attilio Milano, "I banchi dei poveri a Venezia," *Rassegna Mensile d'Israel* 17 (1951): 250–65.

13. ASV, *Senato Terra*, Deliberazioni, 16 November 1558, Reg. 41, fols. 133r–137r; 19 February 1567 (m.v. 1566), Reg. 46, fols. 7r–13r (the banks mentioned are five); Brian Pullan, *Rich and Poor in Renaissance Venice*, Oxford: Blackwell 1971, 528.

San Girolamo canal, near the bridge leading to the campo, the second between the Italian and the German synagogues, and the third near the Agudi bridge.

At Rialto instead, under an archway probably located next to the private banks under the arcades in campo San Giacomo, auctions of unredeemed pawned goods were held. The Sopraconsoli dei Mercanti complained several times about previously agreed on prices at the expense of the "poor": for that reason, crosschecking between Christians and Jews, and between the Venetians and foreigners was necessary.[14]

From the end of the sixteenth century, pawn broking was definitely a service rendered by the Jews, though no longer as profitable for them as it once because of the ceiling to the interest rate practiced imposed by the Republic. This service was increasingly financed by taxes imposed on Jewish communities (including Sephardim, traditionally traders and not moneylenders), and for that reason it became a factor of internal unity and solidarity and identification contrasting with the external world.

Ultimately, the city's economic organization within the urban structure was made up of two distinct areas of banking activities under public control: that of the Rialto (decided with the establishment of the Banco Giro in 1587 (a public bank created by the Republic of Venice which became fully operational in 1619) to protect the money of businessmen and entrepreneurs and enable cashless payments and money transfers, and that in the ghetto. Well-known, prestigious families operated in two areas: the Priola, Lipoamino, Pisani, and Soprano in the first, and the Anselmo dal Banco, Luzzatto, and Calimani in the second.[15] In 1673, an illustrious contemporary observer,

14. ASV, *Senato Terra*, 3 August 1508, Reg. 16, fols. 25v–26r.

15. Donatella Calabi and Paolo Marachiello, *Rialto: le fabbriche e il ponte*, Turin: Einaudi, 1987, ch. 2; Frederic Ch. Lane and Reinhold C. Mueller, *Money and Banking in Medieval and Renaissence Venice*, Bal-

Simon Luzzatto, stated that Jews paid the State 250,000 ducats a year and employed at least 4,000 Christian craftsmen for the movement of goods sent out to other parts of the world.[16]

In the seventeenth and eighteenth centuries the banks, like other business set up in the ghetto and also used by Christians, lead to the opening of doors overlooking the canals, along the outer perimeter—accessible all hours, even when not permitted—as well as the construction of new holes in the wall. They resembled shops open to the public in existing buildings, with offices on the ground floors and cashiers and registers upstairs. The shelves placed next to partition walls held not only the pledges (those not redeemed were sold at the Rialto, in the presence of a notary public), but written terms of the loans. With a unified organizational structure, each governed by six attendant ministers (three in charge of collection and storage of goods, the other three of registration), the three banks established in 1591 survived, dominating the campo del Ghetto Nuovo up the fall of the Republic and the elimination of the ghetto itself.[17]

RESPECTED PHYSICIANS

"Among the professions ... only medicine was accessible"said Marin Sanudo: it is assumed that in a hundred years, between 1517 and 1619, graduates in medicine at the University of Padua included eighty Jews (a large number at the time). Famous Jewish doctors gave some courses and lectures, among them Elia del Medigo, of Cretan origin, whose pupils included Pico della Mirandola. There was Abraham de Balmes, from Naples, one of whose followers and students of Hebrew was

timore: John Hopkins University Press 1985, 76–79.

16. Luzzatto, *Discorso circa lo stato*, 28ff.

17. ASV, *Senato Terra*, 31 January 1597 (m.v. 1596), Reg. 61, fols. 165v–172v.; 16 November 1624, Reg. 94, fol. 238v.

Cardinal Domenico Grimani. Other physicians emigrated to the lagoon from Spain or Portugal; some were given tasks of trust, even poisoning the politically awkward figure Hieronimo Adorno on behalf of the Consiglio dei Dieci.

As experts of the healing power of herbs, waters, ways of preventing the plague, the importance of airing, living conditions in the city and countryside or the risk of famine, the physicians' role was unanimously recognized. It was well documented in pages of some travelers, such as Marin Cavalli (1567), and in the description of *caravanserai* (where Jews were often present) met on the way to Constantinople, but also in the admissions of *baili* as famous as the future Doge Andrea Gritti and his son Alvise.[18]

Forced to live in the ghetto when the boundary was set up on July 29, 1516, physicians were, however, given permission by the Senate to go out at night to participate in scientific meetings or cure the sick, although the following year the Consiglio dei Dieci decreed that they were not allowed the privilege of dressing like nobles, a prerogative instead of their Christian colleagues.[19]

SHOPS AND BROKERAGE HOUSES

Workshops and offices were set up, not only around the campo of Ghetto Nuovo, but particularly on ground floors, taking advantage of the shape of the square: doors and gates were opened, mainly along the boundary canals, along with balconies, terraces, *liagò*, and altanelle overlooking them, a clear

18. Achille Olivieri, "Il medico ebreo a Venezia," in Cozzi, (ed.), *Gli Ebrei e Venezia*, 450–68; Nelli Vanzan Marchini, "Medici ebrei e assistenza cristiana nella Venezia del Cinquecento," *Rassegna Mensile d'Israel* 45, nos. 4–5 (1979): 139–41.

19. Sanudo, *Diarii*, Vol. 22, 24 April 1516, col. 162; 29 July 1516, col. 392; ASV, *Provveditori alla Sanità*, Capitolare II, b.3, fol. 14r; ASV, *Consiglio dei X*, Misti, Reg. 41, fol. 4r.

sign of how private space—both water and pedestrian ways—intruded on public land. The type and materials used for these appendages outside the surrounding walls were similar to those used in buildings elsewhere in the city. Regulations aside, there were many examples even in this area: on the one hand they allowed expansion of an excessively narrow residential space, on the other they met the need to open up towards the urban setting and entertain relations with it. In 1647, the magistrates reminded the populace that wooden platforms, justified by the lack of space of the living quarters, and now a place where goods were displayed were not to be used for bargaining. These transgressions, however, demonstrate a very different appropriation of the city space from that set out in the official resolutions: of the 250 units surveyed in the area by the Dieci Savi alle Decime in 166, a full 62 had a *altana, altanella,* or terrace, most overlooking the canals.[20]

A particular profession also developed, that of *senseri,* business brokers, who ended up playing a primary role in movement and use of places of business in the ghetto. Brokering was linked not only to the limitations imposed on citizens and foreigners, but also to the type of product sold and the space where the *negotio,* negotiations, took place. Authorization to open a brokerage shop was recognition and a privilege regulated like membership of a corporation, offered by the Republic mainly to Christians, but also to a large number of Turks[21] and some rare Jews, of particular worth for the State, and consequently sometimes free—like physicians—to move around the city.

20. ASV, *Ufficiali al Cattaver,* 27 July 1594, b. 244, Reg. 5, fols. 121–122; 27 October 1594, b. 244, Reg. 6, fols. 128r–129r; *Savi alle Decime* 1661, b. 426, Condizioni aggiunte 1589, 2, b. 181, n. 3416; *Savi alla Mercanzia,* II ser. 24 October 1647, b. 63; Carla Boccato, *Licenze per altane*: ASV, Op. 10349 (with reference to the documents of the Giudici del Piovego).

21. Giuseppina Minchella, *Frontiere aperte. Musulmani, ebrei e cristiani nella Repubblica di Venezia,* Rome: Viella 2014, 31–34.

At the gates of the ghetto, at any rate, a multitude of merchants interacted intensely, causing Venetians nobles and citizens to buy or sell in the shops of the Jews, representatives of the magistrates to borrow the decorations needed for festivities and ceremonies, officials to bargain *mercati di gran negotio* (important business deals) in front of special shop windows.

EXCEPTIONS TO THE RULES

On the other hand, the official rules were strict for both Jews and Christians. The Most Christian Guard Corradini for example, who in 1603 obtained a house in San Canciano, was told that he could not establish friendly relations with those he was supposed to control: his windows allow him to "see", but the door was only accessible from the outside. And the Sopraconsoli alla Mercanzia could not enter ghetto homes without an explicit mandate, even when called upon to intervene in matters within their competence.[22]

Conversely, there are many Jews who, sometimes risking fines and punishment, left the ghetto taking their things to the inns, taverns, the suburban habitation of Giudecca, Castello and Santa Croce, where Christian senseri did not like to venture. Perhaps they managed to swindle poor widows, courtesans, naive children—as some contemporary documents complained—but they probably served the least well-equipped parts of the city. Certainly, around the middle of the sixteenth century, the owners of shops at the Rialto went to noble houses and those of Christian citizens to show and sell their wares, while a hundred years later only the twelve Jewish senseri in the ghetto were free to circulate, being members of the art.[23]

---

22. ASV, *Inquisitori agli Ebrei*, 22 October 1603, b. 19, fol. 457.

23. ASV, *Ufficiali al Cattaver*, 24 May 1586, b. 242, fol. 104; *Inquisitori agli Ebrei*, 1653, b. 20, fol. 476.

Some of the clauses laid down in the *mariegola* (statute) of the senseri, banning going from shop to shop, "reaching out to buyers" or displaying goods, as well as the obligation to trade "in the light of the sun" with doors, shops, wide open balconies and curtains, provide insight into the oriental features of this fragment of the Venetian urban fabric. New immigrants helped transform it fairly quickly in a sort of small caravanserai, full of confusion, colors, smells, noises, swindles, and under the table agreements. But it was also clear that the inhabitants gradually appropriated not only their piece of the city, but the idea of using the entire space, albeit with some limitations of time and quantity of merchandise.

The Rialto was also an attractive location: in spite of the strict rules allowing access in specific days and times, it was popular with those working pearls and precious stones, or who sold fabrics. Moreover, ever since the early decades of the seventeenth century, archival documents clearly show the existence of Jewish shops even outside their assigned area in Cannaregio. In 1636, the jewelers settled in Ruga degli Oresi protested against the presence of Jews, with their own workers and disc grinders, in sale and processing of precious stones; they obtained a decree from the Senate limiting the presence of Jews in this area set aside for the production and sale of jewels. Similar acts were passed for tailors, furriers, and food producers.[24] The Senate resolutions concerning ornaments to be prepared for Easter celebrations, hospitality of prestigious personalities, or for Bucintoro—prepared and loaned by Jewish rag merchants—highlighted the number of shops and stores of these concerns outside of the three ghettos. At the same time, however, Christian citizens were strongly attracted to the ghetto, coming not only for the mentioned services, but also out of curiosity and opportunities

---

24. ASV, *Senato Terra*, 28 November 1636, Reg. 115, fols. 348v–349r and v.

for exchange. In 1589 for the reckless baker Giorgio Moretto of Santa Maria Formosa went into Giacomo de' Cresci's bakery to bake unleavened bread, although aware of the risk of a trial and a heavy punishment.[25] The incident is not isolated.

On the other hand, we know that Christians attended parties and dances organized by the Jews in their homes and, conversely, that Jews could be found in patrician palaces, even for many nights in a row. Some of the ghetto inhabitants were dancers and thespians, and music teachers of Christian nobles, although it is likely that cultured musical compositions only entered Venetian synagogues at the beginning of the seventeenth century. We know that there was even a theatrical entrepreneur among Venetian Jews, Josef Camis, an eminent physician and scholar of philosophy in relation to some Venetian nobles active in the opera house.[26]

These "abusive" professions, widely practiced and sometimes even permitted, almost expressed a desire to encourage the meeting of nobles (citizens and foreigners) and "knowledgable" people to protect what was a difficult balance but, one pursued persistently by the Republic magistrates.

25. ASV, *Santo Uffizio*, proc. A Giorgio Moretto, 8 April 1589, b. 64.

26. Beth L. Glixon and Jonathan E.Glixon, *Inventing the Business of Opera: The Impresario and his World in Seventeenth Century Venice*, Oxford: Oxford University Press 2006, 82 (thanks to Gabriele Mancuso for pointing out this occurrence to me).

Maps of the Ghetto Nuovo with the sites
of the five synagogues: 1. Tedesca; 2. Canton;
3. Italiana; 4. Spagnola; 5. Levantina.

(Graphics by Alessandra de Ferrighi)

⤳ 5 ⤳

RELIGIOUS LIFE

In Jewish tradition, the synagogue is a religious and cultural center, a place of study, the house of the community. The word derives from the Greek συναγωγή for "assembly" and is a conceptual translation of the Hebrew term *Beit Knesset*, i.e. a "meetinghouse". In sixteenth century Venice (but also in Rome) a synagogue in general was called *Scuola*, from *shul* (לוש) in Yiddish, but was also something of a confraternity, similarly to the Christian *Scuole Grandi* and *Piccole* found in lagoon society starting in the second half of the thirteenth century.

Legally recognized by the Consiglio dei Dieci, the scuole gave material and spiritual assistance, commercial and ethical instruction to its members, and defended common interests. They were devotional or craft associations, created with religious purposes, but also for social services and solidarity, governed by elected lay officials. The scuole provided charity, and helped build apartments to rent, hospices for the needy, and hospitals for the sick. From the time they were first founded, they were an important element of balance between the different classes and professional components in Venetian society, and—in some cases—have survived to the present day. Each scuola had its own special venue, supported by the members' contributions and bequests and was regulated by a statute or mariegola. They were housed in buildings whose marble facades, monumental staircases, and the decorations and paintings of their salons used for meetings (the *alberghi* [hotels]) were of exquisite artistic design, especially in the fifteenth and sixteenth centuries.

A significant variation of these organizations was found in the national scuole for specific groups of immigrants. They offered a segment of the city's foreign population a sense of belonging, organized and protective vehicles for alien merchants who came to Venice on business to trade with the city's citizens. Each group—Lucchesi, Milanese, Bergamaschi, Friulians, Florentines, Albanians, Schiavoni (or Dalmatians), Greeks, and Germans—had their own scuola.

INVISIBLE SYNAGOGUES

Before the Jews were enclosed in the ghetto, Jewish prayer services took place in private homes, near the Rialto before the ghetto, and inside the enclosure for at least a decade when—as we know—the 1516 Senate decree prohibited formal prayer gatherings. There is testimony of this practice from 1408 when the *visdomini* of the Fondaco dei Tedeschi (Venetian officials in charge of Fondaco operations) complained that the Jews set up synagogues in the Christian homes they rented and there organized religious rituals (*quod iudei in domibus christianorum quas tenant ad affictum faciant sinagogas et dicant intus offitia sua iudaice*).[1]

Starting in 1528, places of worship were established in the Ghetto Nuovo, not far from the passage that connected the campo with the Ghetto Nuovissimo, although they were still prohibited. On the other hand, there was no outside indication of their existence.

The first real synagogue was built the same year by the Ashkenazi community, "under the protection of the Lord" as an inscription there reads. It was used to celebrate religious rites, but was also an organizational, social and educational reference point.[2] In the sixteenth century, the new Scuola Tedesca

---

1. ASV, *Compilazione Leggi*, b. 189, no. 48, 5 May 1408 (Capitolare dei Visdomini del Fondaco dei Tedeschi).

2. Giacomo Carletto, *Il ghetto veneziano nel '700 attraverso i catastici*, Rome: Carocci 1981, 47–52.

was a large prayer and meeting hall on the third floor of a building between the river and the square owned by Valier. It was reached via several flights of stairs. Just four years later (1532) the Scuola Canton was also established nearby on one side of the campo (in the corner, *canton* in Venetian) on land owned by patrician Erizzo family. The Scuola Canton was also Ashkenazi and was located on the third floor of the building. The Italian Synagogue, the third to be established, was close by and also overlooked the campo of Ghetto Nuovo. It was probably established before 1566 and then remodeled in 1575 in a building owned by the Da Brolo family "which was intended as an attic". The Scuola Italiana was a garret renovated to accommodate one prayer room and two others in the back. The three synagogues communicated with the residences surrounding them via passageways between neighboring properties. They were reached via a steep staircase shared with some apartments, reaffirming the sanctity of the high sites and thus the value of religious symbolism.

All three synagogues were a confirmation of one of the rules set down by Talmudic sources and biblical literature, i.e. that the places of prayer should rise over the city and be reached by going upward. Above all however, they were not located in Christian owned property, but in the part of building of "additions and improvements" made by Jews and therefore subject to more direct control of the Jewish community. Preventive protection from potential conflicts and possible interference, a psychological feeling of possession, practical sense were all equally pivotal factors in the decision to locate the synagogues on the upper floors. So much so that, despite reiteration of the need for more space, nothing higher than these three synagogues was ever built.

Further confirmation of the rule of the synagogues' elevation came with a 1667 agreement between the deputies of the Italian school and Letizia Attias, who lived next door. Like the dispute in Ghetto Vecchio the previous year between the Scuola Spagnola and a certain Nascimben Nasi to stop the work he started in an attic, later acquired by the school itself, the agreement reiterated the requisite to observe the 'tradition' that synagogues overlook the city.[3]

In these very simple constructions, organized within a group of houses and—contrary to Christian churches—without any ostentation or formal embellishments, the presence of light was a fundamental element: natural (thanks to large windows and skylights) and artificial (with large candelabra). Light was life, security, and peace. The first synagogue, the Scuola Tedesca, included a precious façade with mullioned windows, now partially blocked, which took up the entire wall in the prayer room facing the campo, and let in considerable light, along with a central skylight (recently covered). Whether the mullioned window pattern reproduced features of Venetian civil architecture—as theorized by Sebastiano Serlio—or those in some Renaissance buildings (as some scholars have noted) it is certain that the five large windows (detached rather than touching) also reappear in façade of the Scuola Italiana. The skylight, a sort of open dome, is replicated in both the Scuola Canton (fig. 11) and Scuola Italiana.

Ultimately, the three major and three minor synagogues placed along the outskirts of the Ghetto Nuovo had important social and religious roles in defining the open space as a place of collective identity. At the same time, they spoke a subdued architectural language with their external façades, but with rich interior decorations refurbished and embellished, stratified over time, and closely connected to nearby lodgings by way of adjacent access.

---

3. Ennio Concina, "Parva Jerusalem," in Ennio Concina, Donatella Calabi, Ugo Camerino, (eds.), *La città degli Ebrei. Il ghetto di Venezia, architettura e urbanistica*, Venice: Albrizzi 1991, 93–155; see also the quoted documents and lengthy bibliography.

Conditioned by already existing constructions, the Scuola Tedesca is trapezoidal; it was altered in the seventeenth century on the model of the Venetian School and again more recently, partly to arrange it on bifocal plan with the *bimah* (pulpit, near the wall overlooking the campo) and the *aron ha kodesh* (ark, or cabinet of the Torah scrolls) at opposite ends. The ark protruded slightly from the outer wall over the rio degli Agudi, a *liagò* (as these small, external loggias are still called in Venetian dialect) frequently found in buildings throughout the city, and also in the neighboring synagogue Canton. Instead, in its sixteenth century plan, the building probably had the typical central European Ashkenazi pattern with the bimah in the center under the skylight, the model for the Scuole Canton and Italiana. Later, the *aron* became a refined niche with Corinthian columns, raised on four steps of Verona marble and topped by a broken pediment with allegorical elements of decoration with clear formal references to contemporary models of altars in Venetian and Veneto churches; the rest of the room is marginally related. It is characterized by an overhanging ovoid women's gallery, added later to replace the one on the side of the entrance, effective in attenuating the spatial irregularities (fig. 9).

The second synagogue, the Scuola Canton, is located in the south east of campo of Ghetto Nuovo. Its name—highly debated—refers simply to the name of the site, symmetric in addition to another "corner", that of "the *forno*" (oven).[4] It too was used for prayer and social activities. Besides the synagogue, the building also held the Fraterna sive Scuola Talmud Torah di Ghetto Nuovo (the local school of religious studies for children) with a "*logheto*—small room—where teaching took place

---

4. ASV, *Notarile*, Atti, Andrea Calzavara, b. 2993, 24 April 1664; ibidem, b. 3002, fol. 99r, ibidem, 23 May 1667; b. 3004, fol. 992r, 21 December 1667; *Savi alle Decime*, Redecima 1661, b. 426, nos. 86-88, 93, 99; ibidem, Redecima 1712, b. 288, cond. 1034.

for Love of God" and, on the ground floor, the coffin storeroom of the Fraterna della Misericordia—Confraternity of Mercy— replaced in the nineteenth century by the Fraterna dei Poveri— the Confraternity of the Poor. Two Doric columns designed in the Lombardos' workshop give us a hint of the sixteenth century arrangement of the vestibule on the ground floor. But the conformation was certainly the result of a long history of modification, along the perimeter as well: in 1638–39 and again between 1657 and 1658 and perhaps in the early eighteenth century when a "place for women" was built.[5] At that time a staircase was removed from the confraternity *midrash* (place of study) leading to the synagogue, making it possible to enlarge and regularize the area for prayer, already organized on a bifocal basis, *aron* and bimah opposite each other on the short sides, unlike the previous Ashkenazi Scuola Tedesca (which was also larger). Here too, the ark was arranged, and accentuated in the façade in a *liagò* protruding over the canal, while the pulpit was located in a bright apse with side windows and domed skylight (fig. 10). It was covered by a lowered arch resting on slender spiral columns with plant motifs, an iconographic theme that has been related to the importance of the vine in the Psalms. Its design has been compared to a famous drawing by Guardi for a Gradenigo family altar. With a clear, more formal change in approach, corresponding to the city's Jewish minority greater sense of security, seventeenth century renovations were not assigned to an anonymous professional, but to Bartholomeo Scalfurotto. He was a fairly well-known architect and sculptor in the lagoon, working for Jewish clients elsewhere, and engaged in those years in building the bell tower of San Pantalon and the restoration of the façade of Palazzo Ducale.[6]

5. ASV, *Notarile*, Atti, Andrea Calzavara, b. 2975, fols. 773r ff., 30 December 1657; ibidem, b. 2976, fols. 45r ff, 12 March 1658, and fols. 315r ff., 11 June 1658; *Savi alle Decime*, Reg. 876, 30 January 1732.

6. ASV, *Notarile*, Atti, Andrea Calzavara, b. 2975, fols. 773r ff., 30 De-

The construction of the Italian School, the adaptation of a garret belonging to the Da Brolo family, was perhaps built before 1575. It was a vestibule near the canal with "space above for women", a large room jointly housed in two adjacent buildings. The promoter, the Magnifica Università degli ebrei italiani (the University of the Italian Jews, the community governing board), was established in Venice in 1555. Additional construction projects were carried out between 1581 and 1587, although access was through the present entrance. In 1609, a master bricklayer and a stonemason reconstructed the masonry and raised the roof, as well as renovating the women's gallery and opening a skylight on the roof (perhaps the dome under the apse which has been compared to the more or less contemporary solution used to light the apses of San Salvador). The hall of worship is an approximate square and conditioned by pre-existing loadbearing structures. Double in height, it is lit on one side by five large windows overlooking the campo (fig. 12), and on the other—towards the canal—by two rows of square windows that corresponded to the women's gallery. It too had a bifocal floor plan; the bimah stood under the apse and the corresponding skylight. Renovations were done on the women's gallery in 1667, and there were three years of carpentry work carried out between 1737 and 1740. The current arrangement, with rebuilt stairs, the reconstruction of windows overlooking the campo, the restructured *aron*, and renovation of wooden altar frontals can be dated to 1808 with designs by architect engineer Pier Angelo Fossati. The ambitious renovations—with four Corinthian columns on high pedestal to hold a massive entablature—might reproduce the previous Baroque style, but as part of a unified architectural project based on updat-

cember 1657; ibidem, b. 2976, fols. 45r ff., 12 March 1658, and fols. 315r ff., 11 June 1658; *Savi alle Decime*, Reg. 876, 30 January 1732.

ed neo-classical language.[7] The special feature of the façade, with a small terrace, and a sort of *tempietto*, probably adapted from a nineteenth-century portico, have no relations to the synagogue itself.[8]

THE SEPHARDI APPEAR

The dates of the two Sephardi synagogues of the Ghetto Vecchio are uncertain. The first reference to the existence of a place of worship in this area is from 1566, when, in their tax declarations, the Minotto alluded to buildings rented to the University of Levantine Jews—the governing board of Levantine Jews. In 1582 one of them mentioned the Scuola che lozza forestieri, i.e. home to a congregation that also provided accommodations to traveling Levantine Jewish merchants. The same year, Luca Malipiero declared that he collected rent "from the synagogue" located in Ghetto Vecchio "in Canton del Forno," lit. the corner of the oven (probably referring to the synagogue of Jews from the west, i.e. mostly Spain and Portugal). However, as early as 1584, their community set up its first *Libro delle parti*.[9]

It is certain that, at the end of the sixteenth century, the two Sephardi synagogues were facing each other in the small campo of the Ghetto Vecchio; no longer hidden because they were authorized *de facto*. There was direct access from the *calle* (street).

---

7. ASV, *Giudici del Piovego*, b. 23, fasc. 16, 12 September 1737; *Procuratia di San Marco de Ultra,* Commissaria Da Brolo, b. 56, fasc. 13, fol. 73, 25 August 1739; *Prefettura del Dipartimento dell'Adriatico*, b. 136, fasc. 3, 1808.

8. ASV, Notarile, Atti, Andrea Calzavara, b. 1340 bis, 2 December 1677; ibidem, b. 3003, fols. 769v–774v, 18 October 1667 and 9 March 1668.

9. ASV, Savi alle Decime, Redecima 1566; b. 131, cond. 924, b. 134, cond. 843; Redecima 1582, b. 160, cond. 782; cf. also Umberto Fortis, *Il ghetto sulla laguna*, Venice: Storti 1987, 67.

The first building renovated, with the aim of increasing stylistic quality, was the Scuola sive sinagoga della nation Ponentina, or Scuola Spagnola. It was much larger than the original synagogue, adjacent to a terrace and private apartments and with an impracticable attic. Sometime before 1612, the Community began negotiations with the owners for the purchase of some houses and a promise that no adjacent apartment would be built on a higher level, to ensure light in the new synagogue. The following year, in order to *slargar la sinagoga*—enlarge the synagogue—a commission was appointed, including among others Juda Camis, intendant of architecture, one of those involved in work on the Ghetto Nuovissimo and in contact with Venetian masters of the era like Antonio Gaspari and the workshop of Longhena.[10] Afterwards, protests, agreements, private agreements with neighbors superseded each other, through a series of admittedly piecemeal measures until the sixth decade of the seventeenth century, led to the completion of the first entirely separate edifice for worship inside the enclosure: a building clearly laid out, with four large windows and the understated entrance portal, comparable to that of the buildings of the Greek community in the Castello sestiere designed by Longhena's workshop, if not by the architect himself. Inside, the synagogue was again set on a bifocal axis between the *aron* and bimah and marked by Ionic pilasters (placed between the window and the window) buttressing a thick trabeation with a balustrade for the women's gallery running around the room (fig. 13). The ceiling was decorated with rich moldings. The formal opulence was obviously the result of the desire to put the rich Portuguese community and its role in Vene-

10. ASV, *Notarile*, Atti, G. A. Catti, b. 3391, fols. 189ff., 7 May 1612; 14 August 1613; 21 May 1616; b. 3393, fol. 19r ff., 21 January 1614; fols. 75v–77v, 6 March 1614; b. 3399, fol. 22v, 11 May 1620; fols. 128r ff., 13 May 1620; fols. 171v ff., 6 July 1620.

tian society on display.[11] References to the Vendramin chapel of San Pietro di Castello (1642), a tomb in San Giorgio Maggiore, the Sephardic synagogue in London (1674) and the Portuguese synagogue of Amsterdam (1675) suggest that Giuseppe Sardi worked on the synagogue. In those years Sardi was also involved in the designs of the Scalzi church, Palazzo Savorgnan and Palazzo Flangini in San Geremia, all buildings of a certain architectural renown and located in the same *sestiere*. The spatial pattern, designed for a multifunctional complex, intelligently reproduced the organization of the Venetian synagogues discussed above: community and cultural practices (in the synagogue), managerial (in the hotel) and charity (on the lower floors). They were connected to each other vertically by a more or less monumental staircase. This scuola was renovated several times throughout the seventeenth century. We know that initial access to the women's gallery was by an independent staircase, that the same level was an "*andedo*—vestibule—where children study", but the establishment also included the spaces below: a cellar and basement. The congregation also owned a warehouse in court Rodriga, communicating with the Bagno del Rodriga (the only *mikveh*—ritual bath—in the Venetian ghetto of which we have knowledge).

The building of the Scuola Levantina (fig. 14) starts at the Orto court and faces the Scuola Spagnola. Starting in the last decades of the sixteenth century, the rooms, vaults, workshops and warehouses rented to a group of Levantine wayfarers, with a hall to conduct business and the Hospital of the Sick, were renovated to create a synagogue on several levels, including an overhanging women's gallery and rooms below (where "leggono li putti", the children's reading area) used as a school for children. There was a small, adjacent courtyard

---

11. Concina, "Parva Jerusalem," 128–133 and notes 47–52.

where the Levantine community celebrated the festival of Sukkot (or Tabernacles). There seems to be documentation that the merchants in question would pass just a few months in Venice.[12] In other words, they were perceived by the public as "foreigners." This might in part explain the autonomy of the building, completed in stages between 1661 and 1683, but according to a single design. Unlike the earlier synagogues in the Ghetto Nuovo, the building was clearly identifiable on the outside, like in Amsterdam not long before with the Ashkenazi (1670–71) and Portuguese (1671–1675) synagogues.

The close relations between Venice and Amsterdam were testified to in the descriptions of Rabbi Yaqob Rafael Saraval. In one of his letters from the Netherlands in 1771 (he also visited in 1737 regarding a loan request for the Venice Community), he alluded to the commemoration of the centenary of the Portuguese School, stating that "it can only turn out supremely magnificent and corresponding to their good taste and elegance", while he referred to the synagogue as "one of the most beautiful buildings in Amsterdam."[13]

In Venice, the two free, well-proportioned façades, facing respectively the *campiello* and the calle leading to the Cannaregio canal, mirrored each other. They were arranged horizontally with Istrian stone edging, the intervals of the rectangular windows on the ground floor and the much higher at the level of the room used for prayer. The façades were also emphasized by the oval oculi above and marked by two plain, elegant portals and a rusticated base. Scholars have pointed out that these architectural motifs seem to refer to the

---

12. ASV, *Notarile*, Atti, Andrea Calzavara, b. 2996, 8 June 1665: because "the heads of the Spanish and Portuguese are normally foreigners who live only a few months in this city, nor being them stable," a proxy must be nominated.

13. Yaqob Rafael Saraval, *Viaggi in Olanda (1737-1771)*, preface by Pier Cesare Yoli Zorattini, Milan: Il Polifilo 2005, XVI.

work of Longhena (although there is no archival trace of the architect's direct intervention of in the building project) or his school, found in some seventeenth-century palaces such as Giustiniani-Lolin and Widman in San Canciano, Marcello on the rio Santa Marina, the Zane, the Savorgnan or the Labia on the Grand Canal. In particular, there are remarkable similarities in the composition of the Collegio Flangini, used as housing, place of worship and community headquarters of the Greek Community.[14] Inside, the room is not very different from the Spanish Synagogue, although less elaborate and smaller. The same is true of the window frames and portals, as well as the arch that includes a polychrome marble *aron*, also similar to the Vendramin altar by Longhena's workshop. The raised canopy of the wooden *tevah*, or bimah, accessible by two flights of semicircular stairs, was lavishly decorated and supported by spiral columns carved with plant motifs. The triumphal appearance, reminiscent of Bernini, has also been compared to the more or less contemporary altars of the Church of the Scalzi and that of the Jesuits.[15] The spiral column seen in stage sets and a number of Venetian paintings, and in Rome in the same period, was considered a relic of the Temple of Jerusalem, in addition to a sort of citation of many biblical passages and miniatures by Jean Fouquet for *Antiquities of the Jews* by Josephus Flavius.[16]

At the back, along the western wall, there is a windowed apse resembling a *liagò* from the outside (similar to others discussed above, but inverted in the organization of the space).

14. Elena Bassi, *Palazzi di Venezia*, Venice: Stamperia di Venezia 1976; Paolo Maretto, *La casa veneziana nella storia della città dalle origini all'Ottocento,* Venice: Marsilio 1986, 205–212; Concina, "Parva Jerusalem," 136; Rachel Wischnitzer, *The Architecture of the European Synagogue*, Philadelphia: Jewish Publication Society of America 1964, 166.

15. Bassi, *Palazzi di Venezia*, 118; David Cassuto, *Ricerche sulle cinque sinagoghe (scuole) di Venezia,* Jerusalem: Nahon Museum 1978, 51.

16. Wischnitzer, *Architecture of the Synagogue*, 95.

NOT FORGETTING TO BE VENETIAN

Nevertheless, the communities, and their geographical origins, rites, customs were different: they had different liturgies and also a repertoire of melodies that varied not only between Ashkenazim and Sephardim, but also within the latter group. The Scuola Levantina and Spagnola had the same prayer books, but different airs. The music was greatly influenced by the cultural origins of the various communities (Levantini, Westerners, Moroccans, Castilians, etc.). The eastern rite was analogous to all European Sephardic communities, but expressed in a wide variety of liturgical songs, all emblematic of the multiplicity of languages and cultures in the small enclave of Cannaregio.[17]

Ultimately, while the synagogues in Cannaregio all denoted a large amount of structural refurbishing and superimposed layers of decoration, there were numerous similarities to some of the contemporary construction projects in the city. That emphasized the impossibility of isolation, which was not altogether sought out by either the Jews or the Christians. Therefore, the two schools of the Ghetto Vecchio, unlike those of the Ghetto Nuovo, defined their sacred function with autonomous, monumental buildings. In addition, they were much the result of a fusion of Jewish and seventeenth-century Venetian artistic culture, clearly revealing a new relationship between client and architect even inside the enclosure.

17. As clearly demonstrated in the conference: *Genesi, storia e sviluppo della tradizione musicale ebraica in Italia*, Venice, Fondazione Levi, 22 June 2014.

Giovanni Merlo, *Venetia*, with a perspective of the campo Ghetto Nuovo, place of identity for the Jewish community.
Engraving, 1696.

(Biblioteca Museo Correr)

~ 6 ~

COMMUNITY LIFE

The duty to help the neediest members of society has always been a deeply felt commitment of Jewish communities everywhere, and—as soon as a community, i.e. a quorum for prayer, exists—it acts in solidarity to help the more unfortunate fellow Jews.

Albeit voluntary, the system was so widespread and sound that it supplied real relief services for the Jews. According to Attilio Milan, even pawn-broking was originally created as an act of charity towards other Jews in difficulty. What is certain is that, in addition to schools and *yeshivot* for religious studies, numerous confraternities with charitable purposes were established in the Venetian ghetto to help the needy of the different communities living there. In actual fact, in Jewish tradition, assistance—not only material aid, but also to provide comfort, education, and even honor—given to widows, orphaned children, and travelers has always been considered an act of justice.

EDUCATION

Similarly, the school system was very well organized: the richest families made use of private teachers, while others sent their children (boys and girls) to free schools in their communities: illiteracy was considered inconceivable.

Children started learning at an early age (usually five years)—boys and girls. They studied Hebrew and other languages, as well as well as the Talmud and the Bible. Later, adolescents studied mathematics, physics, natural sciences, philosophy and moral treatises.

In Ghetto Nuovo, yeshivot or study houses were created in the same period as the scuole. Unlike the synagogues,
the yeshivot were smaller, and arranged on the lower floors
along the boundary of the ghetto, like the Yeshivah Cohen-
im or Sacerdoti (named for the families of what was once
the priestly class at the time of the Temple in Jerusalem) in
the Ghetto Nuovissimo. The Luzzatto study houses—probably the oldest (1585)—was located on the left of the bridge
leading over the canal to the fondamenta degli Ormesini and
the Mesullamim was located near the bridge to Ghetto Vecchio. Set up inside private homes, supported by individuals,
similar in some ways to the *chiesiole*—chapels—often located
inside Venetian Renaissance palaces, they were refurbished
several times on the outside and their furnishings renewed
in more or less refined style by modest masons and carpenters under the control of the *proto dei Provveditori de Comun*.[1]
They had a complex story related to their architecture and, to
some extent, cultural practice.

There was also a midrash in the Ghetto Vecchio, which—
like the private yeshivot in the Ghetto Nuovo, was part of the
rhythm of daily life. On one hand, it was a school of Talmud,
and a place of prayer not only on Saturdays and Jewish holi-
days, but also in the morning and in the evening at sunset. In
addition, the concern about details of daily life included—on
the urging of Leon Modena, Simon Luzzatto and Gratiadio
Saraval—to avoid cutting beef or veal until the completion of
religious obligations.[2]

---

1. ASV, *Procuratia de San Marco de Ultra*, b. 55, fasc. 4, 29 May 1685;
fasc, 7, 1687-1689; fasc. 17, 24 October 1697; fasc. 5, fol. 53, 20 August
1698; fasc. 3, fol. 11, 16 November 1718; 1 December 1729; fasc. 6, 12
May 1752; fasc. 7, 16 June 1757.

2. ASV, *Inquisitori agli Ebrei*, b. 20, fol. 264v, 6 October 1633; fol. 262,
14 April 1640.

THE OBLIGATION TO HELP

What is certain is that, along with schools and yeshivot, where religious studies and prayer took place, the charitable confraternities in the Venetian ghetto assisted needy members of the different communities living there. In Jewish tradition, helping widows, orphans and travelers has always been considered an act of justice, not only regards to material aid, but to provide comfort, to teach, even "honor."[3]

In addition to Chevrat Gemilut and Fraterna della Misericordia degli Hebrei Tedeschi[4] (both societies responsible for the burial of the dead), there were other groups including the Fraterna per Maritar Donzelle (which provided dowries for poor girls), those helping orphans (Chevrat Hebra de Cazar Orphanos), or groups under the authority of the Levantine and Spanish (Chevrat Pidyon Shavuim) communities to pay for the release of Jewish prisoners in Italy, Hungary, Poland, and slaves in Malta. There were groups that paid the rent for the dispossessed (Chevrat Somek Nofelim), helped the poor in the ghetto in various ways (Chevrat anave ha'ir), provided assistance to poor travelers (Chevrat tredah Derek) and even gave clothing to those who couldn't afford it. Thanks to voluntary donations, a hospice (*Hekdesh*) provided free accommodation for a few days to the poor in transit in Venice, while the wealthy were housed in a central hotel in Ghetto Vecchio, with the approval of the Esecutori contro la Bestemmia.[5] These groups' welcoming and governing of the passage of "foreigners" in the city was essential in facilitat-

3. Attilio Milano, *Storia degli Ebrei in Italia*, Turin: Einaudi 1992, 111, 459–60.

4. Whose rules are found in: ASV, *Scuole piccole e suffragi*, b. 730, fols. 3–64, 27 April 1713.

5. ASV, *Savi alle Decime*, Catastico 1713, b. 433, no. 197; no. 328 II; nos. 95–96 (for schools and teachers).

ing cultural, and commercial, exchange. In addition to fees paid by community members, confraternities raised funds through individual donations, as well as contributions from other cities.[6]

THE CEMETERY AT THE LIDO

Long before the ghetto came into existence, on September 25, 1386, a notary public attested that two Jews, Salomon of the Santa Sofia district and Crisante of Sant'Apollinare district appeared before the magistrates of Giudici del Piovego. The two men claimed to speak in their own name and for the other Jewish inhabitants of Venice, and had come to ask the Signoria to assign a vacant piece of farmland on the coast of San Nicolò where they could bury their dead.[7] The judges Francesco Vitale and Mark Avonale, in the absence of their third colleague Gabriele Tron, being competent to decide due to their ducal mandate, granted said land, whose ownership was not indicated, and for which no rental fee was requested. Located next to the convent of the same name, the boundaries were set for a distance of *70 passi veneziani* [almost 90 meters, NdT] along the sea and 70 along the lagoon, with a width of 30 passi in the direction of Venice and Malamocco.[8]

6. Cecil Roth, *History of the Jews in Venice*, Philadelphia, Jewish Publication Society 1930, 156–57.

7. Charles Malagola, *Le Lido de Venise à travers l'histoire*, Venice: Marcel Norsa 1909, 32, 117–21; Licia Fabbiani, *La fondazione monastica di San Nicolò di Lido*, Venice: Comune di Venezia 1988, 11–13.

8. ASV, *Giudici del Piovego*, 25 September 1385; 18 January 1390 (m.v. 1389); *Convento di San Nicolò del Lido*, b. 5, processi 17, fol. 7; Gian Battista Galliociolli, *Delle memorie venete antiche profane ed ecclesiastiche*, Venice: Domenico Fracasso 1795, Vol. 2, 283–84; Paolo Candio, "L'antico cimitero ebraico del lido nei contratti fra la Comunità ebraica e il Monastero benedettino di San Nicolò (XIV-XVIII secolo)," *Ateneo Veneto* 178 (1991): 109–39.

Moreover—like centers of the Italian peninsula with other Jewish households—Venice was never willing or able to restrict the right to use of urban spaces burial. The choice of location was not easy, but could not be circumvented by those in power. The land to use as a cemetery was also the only immovable property that the Jews could hold: while Christian burial was often intramural, for the Jews it generally took place beyond the borders of the city, in fallow, unfenced land.[9] The plot granted by Venice, more or less rectangular, an area of about half a hectare, was located in a zone at the far end of the non-urbanized, island of Lido, planted with orchards and vineyards, an area also including the properties of Badoer, the Dandolo, the Falier and Morosini, located near the ancient Benedictine monastery of San Nicolò di Mira. The land allocated to the Jews was probably not far from an old Protestant cemetery, most certainly near the harbor mouth, the castles dominating it and the house of the Consiglio dei Dieci. It was also in the proximity of the transit of ships between the open sea and the lagoon, so that in later centuries, the Republic reserved the right to request use of the land at public ceremonies or during the reception of important personages.

As mentioned above, in 1385 a charter was signed between the Senate and Jewish moneylenders from Nuremberg. In the terms of acceptance of the Jewish minority in the city, there was certainly a correlation between the two decisions, close together in time.

For about three years, due to boundary issues, a dispute continued between the monks and the Piovego. The problem of the present and future possession (or perpetual lease) of the land allocated by the magistrates and the intended use of the cemetery was only resolved on February 27, 1390 (1389

9. Andrea Morpurgo, *Il cimitero ebraico in Italia. Storia e architettura di uno spazio identitario*, Macerata: Quodlibet 2014, 19–20, 94–97.

according to the Venetian calendar) with recognition of the Jewish community, represented by Simone and Solomon. In the meantime, the casa di Zudei (house of the Jews), that is the one floor guard house of masonry and timber, covered with tiles (two bedrooms and a kitchen with cabinets and shelves) was added (fig. 16). Jews were not however to claim any right to the north, between this area and the convent, and indeed (and this was the quid pro quo) had to pay for the maintenance of the existing wooden palisade to protect the shore from erosion along the lagoon.[10] The following year the Piovego gave permission to surround the place with a hedge, preferably with a trellis, to prevent vandalism to the graves (*enorma quae fiebant ad corpora judeorum*).

When, with the 1394 charter, the Senate limited the Jews' stay in the Rialto area to fifteen days, they moved mostly to Mestre, where they also found land for burial.[11] The seldom used cemetery on the Lido remained for the use of "wanderers", merchants of passage in the lagoon with doctors' authorization to reside there. However, with the renewal of successive charters (starting in 1508) and the progressive resumption of Jewish residence in Venice, the Senate also reconfirmed use of the land on the Lido.[12]

Finally, after the establishment of the ghetto in 1516 and its extensions in 1541 and 1633, the Università degli ebrei presented a request to the Republic to enlarge the cemetery area, to cope with demographic growth and the effects the plagues in 1575–77 and 1630–31. What is certain is that in

---

10. Carla Boccato, *L'antico cimitero di San Nicolò di Lido a Venezia,* Venice: Comitato per il centro storico ebraico di Venezia, 1980; ASV, *Convento di San Nicolò del Lido,* b. 5, processi 17, fols. 7v–9r; see also Flaminio Corner, *Ecclesiae Venetae antiquis monumentis nunc etiam primum editis illustrae ac in decades distributae,* Venice: 1799, Vol. 14, IX, 119–20.

11. Candio, "L'antico cimitero ebraico," 114, 134n29.

12. ASV, *Senato Terra,* Reg. 16, fols. 42v–43v, 3 August 1508; *Compilazione Leggi,* b. 188, fols. 384r–386v, 19 December 1548.

1578, the Benedictine monks welcomed the call for a "*pe-tium terreni*" adjacent to the existing cemetery. This time, the grant was made in emphyteusis along with a vegetable garden and a boathouse (to "*montar et desmontar*" from their boats) to a Sacerdoti, a Grassini and Luzzatto, who accepted it on behalf of the Università degli Ebrei in exchange for five ducats. New agreements were concluded in 1593, 1621, 1631, and 1640.[13] On the eve of the great plague of 1630–31, there were about 3000 residents in the three ghettos;[14] the epidemic caused the death of 454 Jews, with a mortality rate of 15-20% (compared to 33% of the non-Jewish population of Venice). Witness to the dramatic situation was the inscription "1631 Hebrei" on a gravestone, probably indicating a mass grave, used in those circumstances.[15]

The lands of the Cassinenese Benedictine monks—the monastery was the largest landowner on Lido—were leased to farmers on a long-term basis, with the right to bequeath use of the land to their heirs.[16] The most common contrac-tual formula was emphyteusis: tenants retained their rights even during the Interdict of the seventeenth century (when severe restrictions regarding religious property were in place), provided rent was regularly paid. In the case of the

---

13. ASV, *Convento di San Nicolò del Lido*, b. 5, processi 17, fols. 1, 3, 5, 11, 12v, 13–14, 16v–22, 24 February 1578 (m.v. 1577), 29 gennaio 1622 (m.v. 1621), 7 October 1631, 23 September 1640, 20 April 1641; *Inqui-sitori agli Ebrei*, 1589–1658, b. 45, fol. 372v.

14. As always, census data from the Ancien Régime are controversial: this particular number concerning the plague's death toll is probably more accurate than those supplied by other bibliographical sources.

15. Daniele Beltrami, *Storia della popolazione di Venezia dalla fine del secolo XVI alla caduta della Repubblica*, Padua: Cedam 1954, 58; Sergio Della Pergola, "Aspetti e problemi di demografia degli ebrei nell'epoca preindustriale," in Gaetano Cozzi, (ed.), *Gli Ebrei a Venezia*, Milan: Edizioni di Comunità 1987, 27–28.

16. Paolo Candio, *Note sull'orticultura lagunare nel sec. XVII*, thesis, Università di Venezia. 1985–1986, 4–5.

Università degli Ebrei, the contract was renewed every twenty-nine years: in addition to the rent, tenants made an in-kind contribution (2 capons, a candle weighing a few pounds, or a sum of money to be delivered to the sacristy of the monastery church) and paid a *gravezza* (levy) that the Fraterna della Misericordia whose task was to "oversee the cemetery and the burial of the dead",[17] pledged to declare to the Savi alle Decime.[18]

Over time, the property was used for funeral assistance: vigils over the deceased, burial, and prayers. There were tombstones with family crests, biblical figures, sophisticated monuments with triangular pediments, arches inscribed between pillars, or curved pediments and inscriptions in Venetian, Judeo-Spanish, or Portuguese—again witness to the mixed ethnicity that characterized the Jewish presence in the city and resisted the centuries. These superimposed traces, which according to tradition were elements of "communion between the living and the dead" so that the cemetery itself was called "house of life" or "house of the living",[19] were signs of long-term organized habitation. Given the few remaining documents, the cemetery provides us with valuable information about the shape and growth of an urban infrastructure of the utmost importance. Cultivated with orchards and vineyards, like the neighboring estates of Benedictine friars, in 1593 the cemetery was rented for 25 ducats by the Confraternity of Mercy to a farmer, along with a canopy of marble columns, beneath which was an

---

17. Adolfo Ottolenghi, Riccardo Pacifici, "L'antico cimitero ebraico di San Nicolò di Lido," *Rivista di Venezia* 7 (1929): 3–12.

18. ASV, *X Savi alle Decime*, 1661, bb. 221, 460, fol. 248v.

19. Milano, *Storia degli Ebrei in Italia*, 452–53; Peter Drevins Driscoli, *La casa dei viventi. Un cimitero veneziano*, Sommacampagna: Cierre 1991.

outdoor living space, paved in brick and containing a well.[20] In the contract, signed on September 20, 1609, the gardener Francesco Zampieri, of the late Pasqualin, who rented the vineyard and the masonry house near the cemetery and was required to keep it in the same good condition in which were received, was to give the Fraternity an annual rent of five ducats, as well as three melons and a basket of *persici* (peach). In particular, he was obliged to "keep up", "govern", "improve" and not "worsen" the land, preserving the boundaries and "orchards"(fig, peach, pear, apple, and plum trees, laurels, willows and a pergola of vines).[21] The tenant was also required to keep the area clean ("unsoiled" and "orderly"), not to let in individuals intending to carry out acts of "debauchery" and "insolence", to be always ready to bury bodies in the presence of a Chief Executive Office of Health.[22] It was, therefore, a place that had to be productive, maintained and cared for, where the owners reserved rite of passage, and trees had to be removed from time to time to time to make room for burial.[23] In the mid-seventeenth century, the extension of the cemetery—despite its high rental value and the production of "exquisite garden herbs" for the city market—was approximately doubled, having reached a hectare of land and an increased number of fruit

20. ASV, *Convento di San Nicolò del Lido*, b. 35, fols. 10v–12v, 28 June 1593.

21. ASV, *Inquisitori agli Ebrei*, b. 32, fols. 42r–43r; *Notarile*, Atti, b. 3387, fols. 374r–375v; *Scuole piccole e suffragi*, b. 729, fols. 5r–6r, 20 September 1609.

22. ASV, *Inquisitori agli Ebrei*, b. 32, fols. 105r–106v, 20 September 1609.

23. ASV, *Ufficiali al Cattaver*, b. 242, fols. 117r, 224v, 9 May 1632; *Dal libro grande dell'Università degli Ebrei*, fols. 117, 155, 10 December 1632; *Inquisitori agli Ebrei*, b. 32, fols. 105–106, 22 November 1678; *Miscellanea Mappe*, n. 1412, 30 March 1767; *Senato Terra*, Reg. 296, fols. 388v–389r, 16 September 1728; *Provveditori alle Fortezze*, b. 53, fols. unnumbered, 19 November 1728.

trees,[24] perhaps further confirmation of the acceptance of the Jews in Venice.

THE CANAL OF THE JEWS

On the other hand, in this same period, an episode transpired that—more than any other—showed the close operational ties, if not of skills and culture, that in fact existed between the Jewish minority and Venice. The excavating of the canal of the Jews in 1688 was a typical example of the impact that a microcosm such as the set of the three ghettos and its necessary link with the end of the Lido during funerals had on the lagoon and even on major urban routes.[25]

We do not know whether the decision to excavate the canal was only due to the reaction of Venetian experts faced with a plea from the Jews, or perhaps to the suggestion by an engineer in the field of hydraulics of Jewish origin. In truth, in an earlier era, Jewish experts had been consulted by the Senate regarding the diversion of the Brenta. A certain Solomon of "fine" expertise in terms of water levels, for example, had written on the subject. On July 8, 1444, he went on a survey with the Savi alle Acque to design a diversion of the river that was discussed. And his opinion was approved by the Collegio.[26] Now, in the second half of the seventeenth century, the excavation for the new canal was made, granting the request of the University of the Jews for an "'opportunity to take the bodies to their graves" in the cemetery on the Lido, without having to pass under the bridge of San

24. ASV, *Convento di San Nicolò del Lido*, b. 5, processi 17, fols. 18v–20v.

25. Jean Georgelin, *Venise au siècle des lumières,* Paris: Walter de Gruyter 1978, 945n66.

26. Bernardino Zendrini, *Memorie storiche dello stato antico e moderno delle lagune di Venezia e di que' fiumi che restarono divertiti per la conservazione delle medesime,* Padua: Tip. Del Seminario 1811, tome I, Book II, 106.

Pietro di Castello and suffer the insults of the children of the district. Insults against Jewish funeral rites were not an exceptional event, and certainly not only Venetian: Ariel Toaff reminds us that "this strange procession, which accompanied the coffin outside the walls of the city chanting in a language unknown to all, with dirges so different from those of Christian funerals, drew the curiosity of the people, causing spite and irritation".[27] What makes unique it in the lagoon is that the journey was made by boat (fig. 15).

The new canal was a short stretch of water, but which ultimately corrected the entire course of port shipping traffic and the lagoon depth in some parts (fig. 17). Cutting an opening through a piece of the gardens of the Patriarchate, the Canal became a water link between the Rio delle Fondamente Nuove (behind the Arsenal) where it engaged in that of Marani and rio of Scomenzera to the port of San Nicolò.

The canal was built and then enlarged twenty years later. It happened that a short stretch of water, the depth of which also allowed the passage of boats of a certain size, created to occasionally allow an alternative route to the Jewish cemetery, ended up facilitating navigation from the northern part of the lagoon to the open sea. It therefore assumed an important role in the city's network of waterways.

In a site where the morphology changed continuously, with a hydraulic system that was never definitively settled, the canal of the Jews—which became "very deep" in the next few decades—was believed to be the cause of silting in neighboring canals, and in the direction of the port. Between 1725 and 1739, the effects of the excavation seem to have become so worrisome to inspire measures, projects, and articles by Venice's most famous experts in the field of water. Poleni, Margutti, Riccati, and Zendrini compared notes, using drawings

---

27. Ariel Toaff, *Il vino e la carne. Una comunità ebraica nel Medioevo*, Bologna: Il Mulino 1989, 67.

to buttress their arguments, on whether to oppose the "slow and hidden progress" of natural phenomena, once a process has been triggered by man. The question was whether it was worthwhile to "redirect" the canal with adequate equipment (i.e. lower the depth), bringing back to its former state, or discard this hypothesis, consider the state of affairs inevitable, or starting a project with not entirely predictable effects as dangerous.[28]

For our purposes, the episode indicates that a strong, settled urban relationship had developed between the Jewish structures (all three of the ghettos and the cemetery), and the city. The canal was in fact destined to remain, despite the disadvantages, the effective symbol of an isolation, sometimes pursued by both parties and yet never reached (or reachable) in a context where exchange and relationships determined the residents' material life.

THE "NEW" CEMETERY

Of course, a good number of contradictory decisions remained, emphasizing the fact that real integration had not yet occurred.

Between 1671 and 1675, for example, military defense needs in the war against the Turks and fortification of the coast led to a temporary suspension of the use of the Jewish cemetery, even though rent was still paid.[29] The interference between the two purposes, funerals and fortification building, was seen again after some forty years. New agreements

28. ASV, *Archivio Zendrini*, Reg. 4, fols. 94–101, 3 November 1725; Reg. 7, fols. 288–94 (with the history of the canal), 7 August 1731; *Archivio Poleni*, Reg. 3, T. II, 7 August 1731; *Secreta*, b. 2 (1–3), fols. 77, 124ff.; fol. 139, 18 September 1739 (concerning the declarations of 22 September 1731).

29. ASV, *Compilazione Leggi*, b. 189, fols. 264r–265r, 30 November 1675.

were later needed, in particular in 1715 when the surface of the cemetery was seized to build fortifications. In 1728, however, the Senate received a claim for compensation of the Università degli Ebrei by the *Provveditori alle Fortezze*, and then later—on May 23, 1763—allowed the area to be widened even in the face of ongoing disputes with the monks and impositions of the maintenance by the Ufficiali al Cattaver.[30] Coastal needs were also the basis of the cemetery's decline in the second half of the eighteenth century; then, during the French occupation, gravestones and tombs considered an obstacle to the fortifications were removed and the defensive wall demolished.

During the nineteenth century, however, the need for expansion became urgent (fig. 18). More radical solutions were examined; for example, the possibility of acquiring new land elsewhere, in the San Biagio area in the Giudecca, or the San Michele area adjacent to the Catholic cemetery, to which the patriarch agreed on condition that the Jewish confraternity took responsibility for the achievement of a high impenetrable wall of separation. Nevertheless, this solution (which also appears as a project in the in the famous and very detailed map of the lagoon by Auguste Denaix, 1809–1811) was not adopted.[31] Only much later a piece of land of about one and a half hectares, that was purchased by the Bagni del Lido Company, adjacent to the ancient cemetery, but set back from the lagoon front, in the most distant point from the existing buildings. It offers both material and spiritual benefits. The

30. ASV, *Senato Mar*, filza 920; *Provveditori alle Fortezze*, b. 3-5, Decreti, Reg. 4, 260–61, 16 September 1728; ASV, *Genio Militare*, b. 77 (prima serie), fasc. 12, fols. unnumbered; see Candio, "L'antico cimitero ebraico," 128–29 and notes.

31. Alessandra Ferrighi, "Carta topografica idrografica militare della laguna di Venezia," in Donatella Calabi e Ludovica Galeazzo, (eds.), *Acqua e cibo a Venezia. Storie della laguna e della città*, exhibition catalogue, Venice: Marsilio 2015, p. 135.

new and the old area formed a single body, with trees in all directions, confirming the value of a centuries-old settlement. At this point, after full ownership, the right of permanent interment of remains—crucial for a Jewish cemetery—was recognized and which would not have been possible in San Michele or any other Catholic cemetery.[32] In 1923–1924 the entrance, consisting of a large portal with pointed arches on sturdy columns and connected to a boundary wall in brick, symmetrical and simple stone, confirmed the monumental importance of the intended use of these areas with a sober design and great balance.[33] The project was designed by engineer architect, Guido Constant Sullam, who in the same years also designed graves (Rava, Levi, Errera), using a cultivated language, rich in spiritual symbols combined with the aesthetics of Art Nouveau strongly influenced by Viennese culture, also seen in the architect's designs of contemporary villas built on the Lido and other craft works.

The present ancient cemetery is much smaller than the one created after the agreement of 1578. Works by the city in 1925 and then in 1929 when the so-called "new cemetery"—based on the expropriation of a strip of land for the construction of the road along the lagoon—brought to light some 300 long unknown tombstones, deciphered linguistically by Rabbis Adolfo Ottolenghi and Riccardo Pacifici and architecturally by Sullam himself.

---

32. AMV, *Cimitero Israelitico San Nicolò di Lido*, IV, 25, 1865–1869; IV, 1, 33, 1880–1884; IV, 1, 29, 1890–1894.

33. Patrizia Peron, "Profilo d'ingegneri. Nicolò Pietro Piamonte e Guido Costante Sullam," in Stefano Sorteni e Franca Cosmai, (eds.), *La città degli ingegneri*, Venice: Marsilio 2005, 194–95.

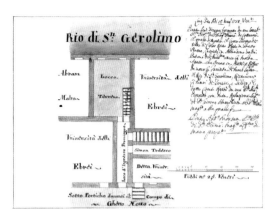

1. Map of the sottoportego leading to the campo di Ghetto Nuovo indicating the location of the pawnshops and the offices of the Università degli Ebrei (ASV, *Ufficiali al Cattaver*, May 18, 1758, b. 278)

2. Hebrew inscription of the façade of San Zulian (1554) during the period when books in Hebrew were printed by Venetian typographers. "Tommaso Filologo (Philologist) from Ravenna, who wrote many books on different sciences and who also found a method to extend man's life over one-hundred and twenty years, had it (the façade) built at his own expense in the year of Creation 5315"

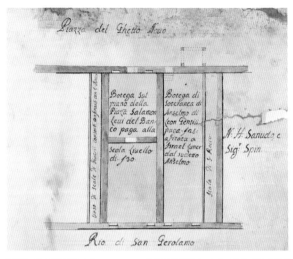

3. Map of two shops on the ground floor of a building located between the Canale di San Girolamo and the Campo di Ghetto Nuovo, property of the Scuola di San Rocco, eighteenth century (ASV, *Miscellanea Mappe*, b. 500, 3, neg. Ds. 46/10, pos. 589, fasc. 1-9)

4. Photo of an *altanella*, overlooking one of the canals in Venice. In the ghetto, the *altanelle*, basically forbidden, allowed their owners to expand their shop and add a shop window to the outside of the ghetto

Facciata corrispondente alla Piazza del Ghetto novo.

5. Façade of an eight-story building in the campo di Ghetto Nuovo owned by the Scuola di San Rocco. Watercolor, eighteenth century
(Giorgio Fossati, *Prospetto verso il Campo di Ghetto Novo delle case di proprietà della Scuola di San Rocco affittate ad ebrei*, 1770, ASV, Scuola Grande di San Rocco, II Consegna, Catastico Fossati, Volume 4, Reg. 29)

6. Section of a building of the campo di Ghetto Nuovo. Eighteenth century watercolor with the internal fragmentation into a large number of apartments, the names of the occupants and the reduced height of the floors all clearly visible (Giorgio Fossati, *Sezione di immobile in Ghetto Novo*, February 6, 1778, ASV, *Ufficiali al Cattaver*, b. 277)

7. Jewish doctor with his patients for a urine exam. Illumination from the *Canon of Avicenna*, translated into Hebrew in the fifteenth century (Bologna, Biblioteca Universitaria)

8. Jewish shop with merchandise displayed on the shelves. Illumination from the *Canon of Avicenna*, translated into Hebrew in the fifteenth century (Bologna, Biblioteca Universitaria)

9. Interior of the Scuola Tedesca with the women's gallery,
the *aron* and the natural illumination of the windows
and the artificial light from the lamps

10. The skylight of the Scuola Canton seen from inside

11. The Scuola Canton with the skylight as seen
from the campo di Ghetto Nuovo

12. Façade of the Scuola Italiana (1566) as seen from the Campo di Ghetto Nuovo: the building is difficult to identify as sacred compared to nearby buildings. Only the five large, second-floor windows mark the presence of this synagogue

13. Interior Scuola Spagnola, with women's gallery: the importance attributed to and artificial light is clearly visible

14. Façade of the Scuola Levantina in Ghetto Vecchio

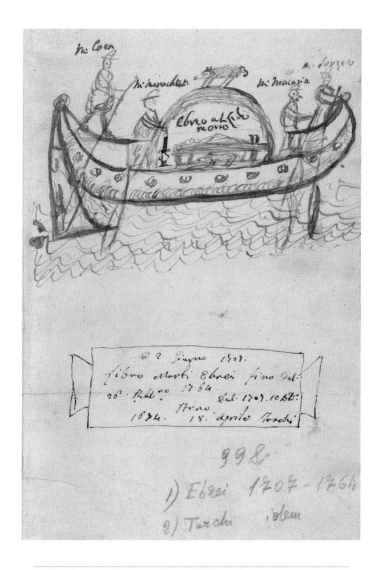

15. Jewish funeral in a boat. Pen and ink drawing, seventeenth century (ASV, *Provveditori alla Sanità*, Obituaries, Obituaries of Jews and Turks, Reg. 998, fol. 1r)

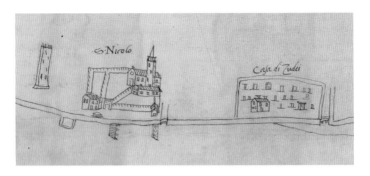

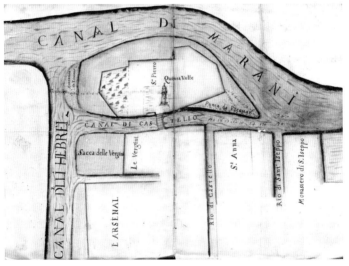

16. Casa di Zudei in the Jewish cemetery of San Nicolò al Lido, facing the lagoon, next to the monastery of San Nicolò. Pen and ink drawing, second half of the sixteenth century (ASV, Anonymous, *Luoghi del Convento di San Nicolò del Lido* [northern shore of the Lido with the "Casa de Zudei"], second half of the sixteenth century, Lidi n° 63, 447,2 x 56,8 cm (neg. 12001; pos.122/I)

17. Daniele Margutti, Map of the network of canals around the Canal of the Jews behind the Arsenale July 27, 1688
(ASV, *Savi ed Esecutori alle Acque*, Relazioni, b. 139, Rel. 9, dis. 1111)

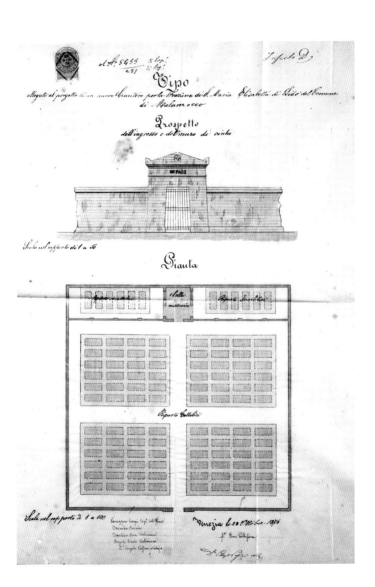

18. Project for the expansion of the cemetery of San Nicolò: layout and
façade of the monumental gate, 1876 (Venice, AMV)

19. Palazzo Treves, façade overlooking the Canale degli Ormesini: the water doors for loading and unloading goods are clearly visible

20. Palazzo Bonfadini-Vivante: frescoes by Giovanni Carlo Bevilacqua in one of the rooms of the palace, c. 1815 (Venice, IUAV)

21. Palazzo Bonfadini-Vivante: frescoes by Giovanni Carlo
Bevilacqua in one of the rooms of the palace, c. 1815
(Venice, IUAV)

22. Giuseppe Borsato, *Sala dei Canova in the Palazzo Treves
dei Bonfil*, Private Collection, 1838–39

23. John Ruskin, *Façade of Ca' d'Oro*. Ink and watercolor on paper, 1845
(Lancaster, The Ruskin Library)

24. Façade of Ca' d'Oro from the Grand Canal

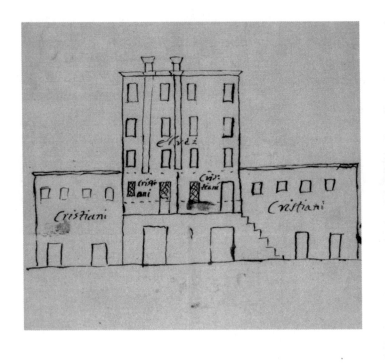

Section of a dwelling in the Ghetto Nuovissimo, by that time Jews and Christians lived in the same buildings.

(ASV, *Ufficiali al Cattaver*, b. 278)

NAPOLEON DEMOLISHES THE GATES

For over two centuries—from the sixteenth to the eigh-teenth—the trades officially permitted to the Jews re-mained limited. At the fall of the Republic, in the Register prepared by Saul Levi Mortera based on direct statements of family heads on October 5, 1797, there were 421 Jew-ish families.[1] The class stratifications remained diversified. Along with a small group of wealthy merchants of Corfu, or Turkish origins, trading large lots of wheat, sugar, oil, colo-nial goods, and draperies in Mediterranean ports, there were eighty-five heads of families generically classified as *senseri di strazze*—rag merchants. They were predominantly brokers who left the ghetto every day to buy or sell at the Rialto— sellers, artisans and agents of the fabrics industry, with an-other forty-seven people performing religious or educational activities and a multitude of servants, maids, and temporary workers.

There were still three banks, employing sixteen people (with different jobs). A first bank crisis came in 1677: the Dominante had made continuous requests for new loans and, in an attempt to correct a difficult economic situation, they had been entrusted the control of the Quaranta al Criminal, who imposed an iron discipline (one Christian scribe and a

---

1. ASV, Saul Levi Mortera, *Anagrafi degli abitanti nel ghetto*, b. 736, 5 October 1797; Gino Luzzatto, "Un'anagrafe degli Ebrei di Venezia nel settembre 1797," in *Scritti in memoria di S. Mayer*, Jerusalem: Fonda-zione Sally Mayer 1956, 194–98; Marino Berengo, "Gli Ebrei veneziani alla fine del Settecento," in *Italia Judaica*, Rome:, Ministero BB. AA., Ufficio Beni Archivistici 1989 (conference proceedings, Tel Aviv, 15–19 June 1986), 9–30.

system of parallel entries). The Università degli Ebrei was declared insolvent in 1721 and again in 1737 and, on that occasion, there was attempt to reduce the number of banks to two, but ultimately, this option was not implemented.[2] Other avenues were also tried, entrusting Rabbi Jakob Rafael Saraval, an educated man of varied interests who lived in the Ghetto Nuovo next to Scuola Canton, with the delicate task of traveling to the powerful Jewish communities of The Hague, Amsterdam and London to ask for loans, given the difficult financial conditions of the Venetian communities. The journey was crowned with success because the communities of Amsterdam and London and the bank of Aron Uziel Hague granted a large loan on favorable terms, considered providential at the time (1737).[3]

Starting from the second half of the seventeenth century, the settlement—which had reached a high building density in both number of units and size of the resident population, the result of two centuries of growth in height and fragmentation—suffered a sharp drop, recorded by the land registry as the number of empty houses or dilapidated and *rovinazzi* (places full of rubble) that caught fire or collapsed.[4] The lives of the three ghettos remained particularly strong however, given the variety of institutions, social structures, culture and trade and, even the realization of a series of new buildings reconstructed on existing houses.

2. ASV, *Savi alla Mercanzia*, b. 63, fol. unnumbered, 9 March 1715.

3. Yaqob Rafael Saraval, *Viaggi in Olanda (1737-1771)*, preface by Pier Cesare Yoli Zorattini, Milan: Il Polifilo 2005, XII.

4. ASV, *Savi alle Decime*, b. 433 Catastico 1713, Ghetto Vecchio; b. 440, Catastico 1739, Ghetto Nuovo; BCV, Donà delle Rose, b. 347, Catastico 1771; see Giacomo Carletto, *Il ghetto veneziano nel '700 attraverso i catastici*, Rome: Carocci 1981, 63–64.

THE GHETTO IS OPENED

Despite the repeated restrictive measures against direct access to the water with "fabricar habitatione—the construction of dwellings—above the embankment of Cannaregio," or the order to place grating along the Agudi canal,[5] new gates were opened and banks to load and unload goods became more common. Pawned goods were moved and stored in more appropriate places (outside the ghetto), as long as proper records were kept. Participation of Christians in convivial events (parties and dances) organized by Jews in their homes and Jewish citizens in the palaces, even for several nights in a row, was a widely practiced form of what was known as "unrest", sometimes even allowed by magistrates who were aware that this helped balance conflicting interests.[6]

The Ghetto Nuovissmo is of special interest in this regard, precisely because it emphasized a transition in the use of land that went far beyond the existing rules. As early as December 12, 1554 (i.e. prior to the establishment of the Ghetto Nuovissimo) the sale of a portion of vacant land in the district of San Marcuola, between the Ghetto Nuovo and the Rio San Gerolamo (the area of the future Ghetto Nuovissmo) by Isabetta Baffo, daughter of the late Vettore Gerolamo Boniperto of Novara, demonstrates the progress of housing development, i.e. the creation of a *calesella*—a narrow street—that reached the canal, of the width required for the use of her land, to be left to the seller. This document preceded a sworn statement of June 6, 1686 and part of the Marcello Commission report of September 12, 1712, accompanied by two wa-

---

5. Carletto, *Il ghetto veneziano nel '700*, 70–71 and the documents cited in notes 44 and 48.

6. ASV, *Ufficiali al Cattaver*, b. 129, fol. unnumbered, 14 April 1723; b. 130, fol. unnumbered, 9 June 1728.

tercolor plans, respectively of the status quo and the subdivision project carried out. These documents showed that the Ghetto Nuovissimo was also granted use of a water gate (as well as the land gate) similar to that of contemporary patrician palaces, later granted to the owners of one of the largest buildings, the Treves de Bonfil.[7]

Gradually over the course of the eighteenth century, on the other hand, the process of social, as well as physical assimilation continued. The Jews' accepted presence and freedom, while at times still needing defense, no longer seemed to be challenged.[8] That is, there were social or business relationships, or only modest real estate activities, indicating that the situation was dynamic, and that there were numerous inclinations towards integration. Back in 1739 the Senate, instituting an exceptional law for exemption for some of the higher-class Jews from wearing a special hat, now black, basically decreed internal community discrimination. Expressions such as "separate Jews"—alluding to changing psychological attitudes—came into use. Among the "separated" some, richer than others, now lived outside the ghetto, like Salomon Treves who, for 500 ducats (a very high figure) rented a beautiful building in San Geremia between 1773 and 1774.[9] Not everything was simple: "the nobility is very divided on the problem of the Jews" emphasized the French consul in Venice in October 1777.[10]

---

7. ASV, *Scuola Grande della Misericordia,* b. 37, Commissaria Marcello, fols. 40–46, 12 December 1554; 6 June 1686; 13 September 1712; 5 January 1713 (m.v. 1712).

8. ASV, *Compilazione Leggi,* b. 189, fol. 489, 10 August 1713; b. 189, fols. 691–692, 8 April 1732; *Inquisitori agli Ebrei,* b. 26, fol. 481, 23 December 1746.

9. ASV, *Savi ed esecutori alle Acque,* Reg. 144, fol. 12, 1773; Reg. 131, fol. 97, 1774.

10. BMC, *Ms. Donà delle Rose,* fasc. 1, Ebrei, 442; ASU, *Fondo Manin,* Ebrei 155/A; ANP, *Affaires Etrangères,* b. 1, 1180.

At the same time, travelers' accounts recalled the "special nature" of the ghetto ("a cluster of eight story houses (above ground level) poorly reduced due to the narrowness of the site").[11]

But that Jews rented rooms outside the areas intended for them in Cannaregio, in order to perform their negotiations, was a known fact and one which the Ufficiali al Cattaver could only "monitor," or "direct by prudence" trying to avoid scandals over cohabitation (still regarded as such). Some attempt to incorporate new buildings in calle della Macina at the beginning of the century and in San Marcuola, just before the fall of the Republic, was accepted with caution by the magistrates, moved "by impulses of piety and zeal."[12]

DILAPIDATED BUILDINGS

What increased or was denounced more dramatically was the number of collapsing buildings, enclosure walls that were out of plumb, bent beams, tumbling fixtures, sloping stone benches, crumbling chimneys, and badly built stairways, in short, dilapidation of buildings and foundations with numerous layers added over time, not counting an increase in actual volume. Without going into detail on the large number of minute operations typical of the time (systematically recorded by the Ufficiali al Cattaver and by the Giudici del Piovego), it is worthwhile discussing one extraordinary intervention carried out in 1757, the subject of a controversy

11. *Memorie sopra le cose antiche di Venezia fatte da Francesco Fapanni, non architetto né ingegnere*, Venice 1886, BNMV, Ms. It., VII 2279 (=9460), fol. 31.

12. ASV, *Savi alla Mercanzia*, II ser., b. 63, fasc. 167, fols. unnumbered, 4 March 1700; *Compilazione Leggi*, b. 189, fol. 414, 21 January 1702 (m.v. 1701); *Ufficiali al Cattaver*, b. 277, 30 May 1780.

that started in 1710 and practically continued until 1826. The work was done in two adjacent buildings in the Ghetto Vecchio, bordering the Scuola Spagnola on one side and the oven and the calle of the same name (calle del Forno) on the other. It involved "fourteen *soleri* (attic or crawlspace) and a belvedere." They were two buildings of seven floors each above ground, timeworn and probably poorly constructed, but in the heart of the Ghetto Vecchio and therefore well located with respect to services (synagogues, bakeries, food shops, and water supply). The two buildings were separated cutting them vertically from each other, to free the proprietary units of a certain number of heirs, that is, to make independent of the apartments that were originally entrapped inside each other. The building complex was cut as if it were a slice of cheese, so as to detach the lodgings on the individual floors and make them easier to rent. The intrusion between the two bodies of the so-called wooden "mad stairs"—and still extant—that even a few years ago required major consolidation, difficult to implement because of possible damage to the static equilibrium, was emblematic of the process of densification that characterized this area for over two centuries. It was also representative of the need to modernize the area (pavement resurfacing, drainage of the exhaust conductors in the two houses, sharing of costs by renters or owners) that could not remain too "different" from what existed in the city's other *sestieri*.[13]

Restoration was necessary and urgent more or less everywhere: in private homes, shops, and public places. At the same time, it must be emphasized that building instability

13. AIRE, *Fondo Astori*, documents concerning the houses of the "scala matta", n. 70, a 60, e 60, b. 60, n. 60, 22 May 1710, 17 June 1710, 26 September 1711, 12 November 1711, 1752, 1757, 1774, 1775, 1776–1777, 1779, 1799, 14 August 1826, 29 August 1826, 28 September 1826.

was increasingly similar to that found elsewhere in the peripheral areas of the city. The 1793 survey on the pavement of San Marcuola and the ghetto streets, cobblestones and tiles on the embankments, the exhaust ducts, walls, wooden and masonry bridges, signed by architects well known in the city, simply followed a decision made five years earlier by the Senate to draft (*sestiere* by *sestiere*) a public registry of the entire urban complex.[14]

THE GATES ARE BURNED

On October 17, 1797, the Treaty of Campoformio established peace between Austria and France. Five months earlier, on May 16, sixty citizens of the Provisional Municipality signed a Manifesto addressed to the population of Venice, announcing the renunciation of the nobles' right to administer the state and city and delivering the city to the French, declaring the fall of the centuries-old Republic of Venice. The group included three distinguished Jews: Moshe Luzzatto, Isach Greco and Vita Vivante, who evidently considered themselves part of the ruling class and were recognized as such. But this decision was regarded with suspicion by those who still feared harassment and violence, so that Rabbi Jona had to intervene to reassure his friend Jacob Stecher, grand chancellor of the Republic.[15] On the other hand, in early June the Jews were still ordered to continue "with the usual methods and the usual pledges" in the three banks of the ghetto.

---

14. ASV, *Provveditori di Comun*, b. 51 (public registry approved by the Senate on 22 December 1787), 19 November 1793.

15. ASV, Municipalità Provvisoria (1797–1798), *Verbali delle Sedute* (edited by Roberto Cessi), I, part I, XVI–XVII and 605–606; Samuele Romanin, *Storia documentata di Venezia*, Vol. 10, Venice: Naratovich 1853, 152.

The decisive act, however, was in the fifth chapter of the decree approved by the democratic government, "the gates of the ghetto shall promptly be raised so that a separation between them [the Jews], and other citizens of this city shall no longer appear". The implementation of the action was commissioned by the Comitato di Salute Pubblica (Public Health Committee), which was part of the Provisional Municipality. On July 11 of that year, the arrival of Napoleon's troops in the ghetto—renamed "Contrada of the Union"—next to the "tree of liberty" and the burning gates found not only the people, but representatives of the Jewish world. The Jewish leaders stepped onto the *vera* (wellhead) of one of the three wells, and pronounced speeches (one even in Venetian) to enshrine the ghetto's reunification with the city and their own citizenship.[16]

The Jews solemnized elimination "of any sign of the abhorrent separation" by the distribution of 314 ducats to the poor of the parishes of San Geremia and San Marcuola. And so, the "Jewish citizens" gathered in the Scuola Spagnola, with a gesture of charity that was doubly symbolic, because it addressed the "poor" of other faiths, in nearby churches, emphasizing civil reunion, indeed a "happy regeneration of this city."

And then, when Morosini put a corps of Schiavoni (Dalmatian soldiers) in charge of the city, even the ghetto became part of the urban fabric needing security. But complete reconciliation was still to take place and the existence of "separate people" fed a partial climate of anti-Semitism.[17]

---

16. BMC, *Gazzetta Veneta Urbana*, no. 35, 440–41, 12 luglio 1797; Rapporto di Pier Gian Maria Ferrari, quoted in Riccardo Calimani, *Il ghetto di Venezia*, Milan: Rusconi 1985, 421–33.

17. *Decreto del Comitato di Salute Pubblica*, 19 messidor, Anno Primo della Libertà Italiana (7 July 1797), reprinted in Adolfo Ottolenghi, "Il governo democratico di Venezia e l'abolizione del Ghetto," *La Rassegna mensile d'Israel* 5, no. 2 (1930): 12–13 (extract).

Nor did the buildings in the ghetto—with their history of inertia and slow minute changes—undergo any radical or sudden transformation. And a climate of political uncertainty remained, while, a year later during the Congress of Vienna, Venice learned that new restrictive measures would be applied in contrast to the freedoms obtained by the Jews. At the request of the Austrian government in 1815, the prefect opposed the restoration of the ghetto, but until then quite probably only a small number of Jewish families had moved away, nor did many Christians move to Cannaregio. In 1818, the Jews' legal status (right of ownership, access to every level of studies, the free exercise of professions and economic activity) was formalized when they were named "ordinary citizens" of Lombardo Veneto. But in the 1830s, there were still indirect attempts to control population growth and use caution in the development of the settlements.[18]

However, the opportunity for Jews to own real estate (with a large part of the population, living in the Jewish quarter for nearly three centuries, suddenly starting to move) was one of the most significant processes of transformation of the city in the nineteenth century.

On the other hand, decisions and practices of consolidation and restoration generally took a long time: aside from the opening of the gates, the Napoleonic regime's first dramatic gesture to eliminate the ghetto, the use of space and transformation of the urban fabric were neither directly nor suddenly affected by political change.

Nineteenth century events that bolstered decrepit buildings located around the campo of Ghetto Nuovo and the Ghetto Vecchio were unique in scope, but not abnormal compared to what happened in other marginal neighborhoods. For a little over thirty years, there were extraordinary

18. Marino Berengo, "Gli ebrei dell'Italia absburgica nell'età della restaurazione," *Italia* 6, nos. 1–2 (1987): 62–103.

public and private investments, particularly significant vis-à-vis the modification taking place in outlying areas. On the other hand, the parallel process followed by the wealthier Jewish families, abandoning the homes of their ancestors, acquiring and decorating the beautiful homes that belonged to the Veneto patricians, ultimately appropriating other parts of the city, was an obvious indication of the redevelopment underway in the central areas. Ironically, in the great diversity of their economic power and social diversity compressed within a community now of about 1,700 people, the Venetian Jews summed up the rapid changes that the housing situation underwent during the nineteenth century more than other groups.

AN INTERMEDIATE PHASE

Starting in the eighteen thirties, the physical nature of the area that, until 1805, was still an enclosure from the point of view of duties and maintenance costs (the Università degli Ebrei being responsible for its upkeep), was particularly precarious, full of "ruinous buildings," in need of "demolition and restoration."[19] That at least is the image given by documents relating to municipal works and warnings that the municipality sent to property owners, ordering them to take action. Not even road maintenance was ever contracted to the Cannaregio *sestiere*, because for centuries the Jews themselves were in charge. But by the time (1818) they obtained the weights and privileges common to other citizens, the above-mentioned Università degli Ebrei "rightly held itself to be relieved of this burden,"[20] so the paving, wells and surrounding bridges the university once had to main-

---

19. Gino Benzoni, (ed.), *1797, Le metamorfosi di Venezia. Da capitale di Stato a città del mondo,* Florence: Olschki, 2001.

20. AMV, *Atti del Comune,* 14 May 1818, prot. 3445/Strade.

tain were ignored. In the first three decades of the century, in short, the area continued to live as in the past, but in a state of especially serious neglect. In front of the campo shops, some fruit and vegetable and fish stands took on the appearance of a market, while geese were still raised there for food and their feathers were used for mattresses and pillows—like in the country. Suffice it to say that even on December 1, 1830, a Dr. Levi provided a list of existing butchers in the ghetto, the number of geese they owned and the number dead (for a total of 1580 animals), asking the president of the Community to take urgent action against an epidemic that could affect "those birds known as geese bred by us in great abundance."[21]

Elsewhere in the city, the French era was partly characterized by the demolition and reduction of minor buildings. In other districts, that is, the conservation, repair, and renovation of buildings for public use, organization of infrastructures, repaving of streets and squares, and restoration of foundations and bridges began in the first decade of the century, and was often completed under the protection of the Austria. In the ghetto, intervention of this kind came later.

THE WIND OF MODERNITY

Meanwhile efforts ensure "hygiene" throughout the urban context could not be restricted, and this was true throughout Europe. The nineteenth century culture of *risanamento* (redevelopment) was fashionable for city centers and the outskirts, with standardizing housing and substantially neutral regarding different ethnic groups. At first the steps were

---

21. Archivio Maestro, b. 202, *Sanità*, 1 December 1830: doctor G. Levi asks the president of the Community to take action given the epidemc that is causing the death of many geese in the ghetto.

tiny, but a wind of 'modernity' even blew through the campo of the ghetto. Thus, the city approved urgent total demolition of a number of dilapidated buildings; the decision were sometimes bureau decisions, and sometimes based on reports from individuals. In the second half of the century, Civil Engineers insisted on expansion of the Israelite cemetery of Lido in the shortest time possible.

In 1829, a survey by municipal technicians showed the state of disrepair of the buildings located along the San Girolamo canal, on the south side of the campo di Ghetto Nuovo (the square at the side where the present old age home is located). When demolition was decreed two years later, the search for the owners was not easy. In 1835, the chief rabbi had to investigate on behalf of the municipal authorities to identify the companies, and their new domiciles, and give notice that the Podestà ordered the buildings razed. [Oppure "be lowered". Da quello che si dice dopo mi sembra giusto "razed", ma abbassare sarebbe "be lowered". "abbassare" è terminologia desueta: usare razed.] When the canal that ran along them was excavated, many of the apartments (mostly two-room and linked internally with other neighboring properties, which had been demolished in the meantime) were now uninhabited. So, while the map of the French land registry (1808–1811) showed the area adjacent to the bridge and entrance arch in Ghetto Nuovo as intensely built up and fragmented, in that of the Austrian land registry (1838–1842) it was almost completely cleared. And nearby, in the space of fifteen years, other inspections certified the state of abandonment particularly along the canal, the opportunity to clear and renovate, and the need for pro quota compensation for those who paid for renovations. In five years, one entire side of the campo (overlooking the canal)—and with this also the traditional closed form of the square—was changing radically. Four or five years after that, on the opposite side, in buildings adjacent to the Scuola Italiana, there were serious "imbalances" in the façade, structure failure of the foundations on the canal, and danger on the wooden bridge where there was "constant and frequent passage."[22] The city threatened demolition here as well should measures not be taken. In this case however it was the owners themselves who requested that the city offices help build what was considered the most important street of the district—the one leading to the only bridge between Ghetto Nuovo and Ghetto Vecchio—"open, airy and sunny."[23] The Agudi bridge (the original is still in wood) thus had new steps, with that gentle inclination "convenient and healthy", usually introduced in "modern constructions".[24]

Continuing around the square, at the Scuola Coanim, and above the old gatehouse at the wooden bridge, i.e. toward the canal separating Ghetto Nuovo from Ghetto Nuovissimo, other buildings (tall and divided into many units inside, but with "rich woodwork and expensive and ornate construction"), brought a city order to brace up the building, ensure stability, remove terraces or completely renovate the façade. Sometimes the city transferred ownership of derelict, long-uninhabited houses to private owners. Here the president of the Jewish Community challenged the extent of the work required, calling accusations of public danger unjustified. And during inspections, the administrator complained, claiming that expenditures for

22. AMV, 1835–1839, *Fabbriche*, x, 6, 46; 1845–1849, x, 6, 16, Parrocchia di San Marziale, Domande Ghetto, Lavori ai fabbricati; 1850–1858, x, 5, 18, Lavori Cadel e case crollanti in ghetto.

23. AMV, 1835–1839, *Fabbriche*, x, 6, 46 ; 1845–1849, x, 6, 16, Parrocchia di San Marziale, Domande Ghetto, Lavori ai fabbricati.

24. AMV, 1835–1839, 1850–1858, x, 5, 18, Lavori Cadel e case crollanti in ghetto.

the restoration of a building "he had misfortune to own" were too high, while the site manager noted that the commercial value of buildings was greatly diminished, because "the better-off households were domiciled outside the ghetto,"[25] or the extraordinary "elevation" of a building made the seventh and eighth floor apartments practically unsellable. Even so, court rulings were in favor of "reorganization". There were small, typical complaints with associated comments about the allocation of costs, indicating however the area's changed status in the urban geography. It no long stood out due of isolation and ethnic segregation but because it was poor, and run-down, with uncomfortable and unhygienic dwellings that characterized it as peripheral. The descriptions that accompany renovations are often very detailed and used to assess the material substance of this commonplace housing.

So there was a need for massive intervention in Ghetto Vecchio buildings constructed in brick, with wooden partition walls, damaged by war bullets, uninhabited and in a state of complete abandonment, full of "scrap" from the razed sections, or derelict and only partly inhabited in rooms that were still standing, or—on the contrary—"crowded and [only for that reason] of no small value."[26] The changes reported in later land registry maps can be explained by the complete demolition of the "building block" in calle Barucchi, the piling of building parts huddled at the back of the Levantine school, consolidation of the foundations and lower floors, the strengthening of

25. AMV, 1850-1858, *Fabbriche*, x, 5, 18; 1855–1859, x, 1, 47, Vertenza tra il Comune e Cadel Sebastiano per lavori d'ufficio Stabili in ghetto (drawings); 1855–1859, x, 1, 49, Cessione fatta dal Comune a Donà Domenico degli Stabili rovinosi in ghetto (drawings).

26. AMV, 1835–1839, *Fabbriche*, x, 6, 18, Ghetto Vecchio demolizioni ristauri fabbricati.

the loadbearing structures, and the reconstruction of large swaths of the façade in the area between the small square (campiello) of synagogues and the corte dell'Orto. Special reconstruction was done in the fondamenta della Pescheria, which reached twenty-eight meters, the height of the eaves (8 floors, as well as the ground floor); as a result, there was a drastic reduction in the number of units (which however remained high). Less visible work, such as the patching of terraces, exterior and interior plastering, construction of "cages" to protect a well, the extension of previous malfunctioning flues to the top floor, the displacement of a wall of resting on a false base, the excavation of underground pipes and subsequent paving all also indicated that the area benefited from heavy investment in construction. So it was a portion of the city settlement, especially in the area between corte Barucchi and corte della Scala Matta, or the nearby corte and calle dell'Orto, extensively remodeled between 1835 and 1854.

AN URBAN AREA LIKE THE OTHERS

When, despite fines and warnings, the owners did not cover the necessary consolidation, the city itself undertook some "slight expenditures" to clear and upgrade existing structures that were used by the community.

For other buildings, scattered in the three ghettos, the municipal authorities accepted the radical restoration proposed only if the joint owners agreed. On the main road towards the Cannaregio canal, the usual speculative mechanisms of the nineteenth century city found a breeding ground in the historic building density and fragmentation. The location was next to the Scuola Tedesca, in Scuola Canton, in the headquarters of the "Da maritar donzelle" confraternity (which provided dowries for poor girls), around the campo—that irretrievably lost its character as an enclosure. And the many engineer drawings and reports in the Municipal Archives, record the speculation effectively.

Even the old wooden bridges were crumbling, and the city Technical Office repeatedly pointed out the risk of their complete replacement given the side effects they might have on the high unstable surrounding buildings with such shallow foundations. Nevertheless, the final decision was for reconstruction: the Neville company, the same one that built the Accademia, was commission to design the project and a budget. The accommodation to insert iron poles in the embankment, support piers, asphalt paving, "Roman" style embankment, and ultimately the design of new, light and decorated iron walkways were a symptom of the climate of urban renewal running through the entire city. So, if the request to fill in the Battello canal at San Girolamo was one ultimately rejected after a change of direction by the Municipality about covering the canals, such decision was related to work being done in many other canals around the city. It was also a part of a general plan for sanitary drainage and a comprehensive program to simplify pedestrian flows.

The work of the Municipality was sometimes driven by specific land and property interests, or linked to individual business activities. More often, however, it appeared simply influenced by the echo of European urban planning calling for rehabilitation of degraded areas, opening up spaces, favoring empty spaces over full spaces, a view of "sanitization" of the old city. These concepts became catchwords that, even in principle, found particularly fertile ground for application in the urban fabric of Cannaregio. Finally, all three ghettos were truly "assimilated", at least in the way renovation was carried out, the fervor in calling for public works, in a situation of permanent negotiation between public and private.

Fumes from the first industrial settlements on the Giudecca, where some Jewish entrepreneurs engaged in the modernization of the city in the nineteenth century settled.

Charles Yriarte (Marquis de Villemin), *Venise à vol d'oiseau*, 1878.

~ 8 ~

LEAVING THE GHETTO

The arrival of Napoleon brought many urban transformations bringing Venice into the Kingdom of Italy, although only for a few years until the Congress of Vienna of 1815 handed it over to Austria. Venice only rose up against the occupying empire in 1848. The revolt was led by Daniele Manin, a Risorgimento patriot, born to a Jewish family converted to Catholicism. Numerous Jews supported the uprising and participated in the provisional government of the Republic of Venice, presided by Manin, but the revolt was crushed on August 23 after a five-month siege. Returning to the city, the Austrians did not forget the Jews' part in the uprising and closely monitored the ghetto: a soldier attended all religious services.

Venice was permanently attached to the Kingdom of Italy in 1866. That year, thirteen Venetians concerned about issues of hygiene and decorum, sent Mayor Giustinian a letter evoking the goals of the city's "future topography." The desire to transform old buildings into "comfortable and healthy" housing for the middle classes, the need to adapt roads and canals to "needs of the times" for "reasons of public utility" corresponded in fact to a generalized demand. And this gave rise to a season of planning for all outlying areas, including the ghetto.

While on one hand, Jews could enter the professions, hold political office, and own buildings and land throughout Europe, on the other the need of their traditional, "different" and isolated neighborhoods to be modernized was now comparable to other town areas. No radical changes occurred because substantial continuity was inherent in the settlement.

The nineteenth century, however, witnessed no small number of transformations, moves, real estate and proprietary shifts, and ethnic reshuffling fully comparable to what happened in the rest of the city.

THE GREAT FAMILIES LEAVE THE GHETTO

As seen earlier, the refurbishing of degraded areas corresponded to the residential displacements of the richest residents and requalification of larger buildings, neglected for years and in need of consolidation and restoration. Of particular interest from this point of view is the exit of several large Jewish families (whose purchasing power was already considerable and grew even more in the years following the fall of the Republic) from the ancient enclosure of Cannaregio, after they suddenly had the opportunity to invest in real estate. At first apparently, Venetian Jews preferred not to stray too far from the places they knew; they left the ghetto but stayed mainly in the same *sestiere*, sometimes not far from each other and especially near the synagogues. Then, with widening interest in the entire city, they looked to the areas of greatest prestige, for instance facing the Grand Canal.

What is certain is that the idea sustained by historians so far—that in 1815 "very few" Jews had "crossed the borders of the ghetto to establish their homes in contact with Christians"[1]—remains a hypothesis to be tested. From the data collected so far, it seems that Venetian Jews made huge investments in the tumultuous real estate market after the end of the Serenissima. Not all the homes purchased were intended to be inhabited by the new owners: many were rented out. Nevertheless, the impression is of a phenomenon of great residential mobility. It is possible to trace the relative

1. Marino Berengo, "Gli ebrei dell'Italia absburgica nell'età della restaurazione," *Italia*, 6, nos. 1–2 (1987): 65.

shift to high quality buildings in the civil registry and ca-
dastral notifications (with the addition of some information
from notary sources) for about fifty years, making it possible
to examine at least sample cases.[2] They provide understand-
ing of the stormy, accelerated changes in ownership outside
the three ghettos and their indirect effects on the old residences of those families that acquired new real estate in the
first decades of the nineteenth century. In particular, three
monumental buildings in Cannaregio (Palazzo Bonfadini
Vivante in fondamenta Savorgnan, the fifteenth-century Ca'
d'Oro overlooking the Grand Canal acquired by the bankers Errera, and the nearby Palazzo Fontana in San Felice
purchased by Sullam family), show three comparable family
stories. These are three cases of investment in the city in
stages, following a choice to leave the ghetto as a place of residence fairly early, perhaps long before the families accessed
the final prestigious venue.

Between 1811 and 1815 Sabbato Vivante, his wife and children, moved into Palazzo Bonfadini, located in fondamenta Savorgnan.[3] Like many other families of the same name,
branches perhaps, the Vivante originated in Corfu and immi-
grated to Venice not long before, in the middle of the eighteenth century. They were active in the maritime trade and
then, with a growing insurance business, soon became part of
the city's Jewish elite.[4] Of strong democratic conviction, the
Vivante were among the suppliers to the French army during
the Italian campaign, publicly applauded the destruction of

---

2. Donatella Calabi, "Gli ebrei veneziani dopo l'apertura delle porte
del ghetto: le dinamiche insediative," in Gino Benzoni, (ed.), *1797, Le
metamorfosi di Venezia. Da capitale di Stato a città del mondo,* Florence:
Olschki 2001, 147–72.

3. *Palazzo Bonfadini-Vivante*, Venice: Arsenale 1995.

4. Cesare Vivante, *La memoria dei padri: cronaca, storia e preistoria di
una famiglia ebraica*, Florence: Giuntina 2009.

the ghetto gates (celebrated on that occasion with the speech of another relative, Raffaello Vivante, quite active in the city administration). With the Treves, their neighbors residing in the two twin buildings of the Ghetto Nuovissimo, they followed Napoleon's triumphal parade with decorated boats and *bissone* (Venetian ceremonial boat).

In 1811, like the Treves, the Vivante still lived in the contrada San Marcuola, in the Ghetto Nuovissimo, with many other relatives, all "shopkeepers," included in the Venetian land registry surveys of 1771 and 1805 and shown to reside at the same address. In 1808, they also had a shop in the Ghetto Nuovo, four warehouses for their own use on the Giudecca, a house and a stretch of land in calle San Salvador intended for rental, but empty at the time of certification. Preliminary perhaps to new investments in fondamenta Savorgnan, they sold another twelve apartments, all outside the Ghetto Vecchio, located respectively in Castello, the San Cancian district, San Giovanni Crisostomo and San Mattio di Rialto. With the transfer, however, the old family building of the Ghetto Nuovissimo was not sold. Inhabited by other relatives and partly leased, in 1841 it provided Sabbato with a fairly modest pension (121.50 Austrian lire). And yet it remained one of the best buildings in the ghetto area, as certified by an engineer Pigazzi, who described it in detail and assessed the rent at a maximum of 450 Italian lire. On the other hand, the Vivantes had already made an extremely innovative choice, back in 1801 (after purchasing the property at public auction with the burden of the casacà) and then again in 1810, entrusting the painter Bevilacqua, later called to work in palazzo Bonfadini, with the creation of frescoes for halls located in the ghetto. Nevertheless, the value of the building diminished daily as was the case throughout the peripheral area of Cannaregio. Meanwhile, with other branches of his family, Vivante gradually became a reputable real estate owner, so that, in addition to the two houses mentioned above, the Austrian Land Registry showed eight other units in Cannaregio and six in Castello.[5]

In Napoleonic records, the newly acquired building was labeled a "rented building with courtyard" and for the first three years the Vivantes lived there as tenants, later buying it with its annexes and keeping the property until 1848, the year before Sabbato died of the plague. The building was located in an area of the city where there were still large vegetable gardens (there was one in the rear of this building), spaces that would gradually be occupied by manufacturing activities. Nearby, for example, other Jewish families, the Corinaldi and Sarfati, worked in glass production; clearly, there were investments in locations used as workshops, as well as residences. Right from the start, Sabbato's seventy-seven-year-old mother, Anna, and his brother Mandolin, a shopkeeper, as well as Sabbato's wife and daughter, moved with him.

They engaged Giovanni Carlo Bevilacqua, an artist who also painted the Treves buildings mentioned above, to decorate the palazzo (figs. 20–21). The subjects chosen were mythological (in the French fashion), and with subjects (like Duty, Law, and Truth) laden with moralism and tied to their culture, even though at times simply based on allegories of eighteenth century Venetian painting (e.g. *Time Unveiling Truth* of the fresco by Gianbattista Tiepolo).

Ca' d'Oro, overlooking the Grand Canal, registered as number 3933, Cannaregio, was a wonderful fifteenth-century building whose façade was decorated and remodeled several times. It remained almost a symbol of Gothic Venice, after a centuries-long history when it passed hands from one Venetian noble family to another. In the early years of the

5. Calabi, "Gli ebrei veneziani," 162–64.

nineteenth century it was apparently divided among many tenants and no longer inhabited by patricians. In 1824, it was purchased by a Jew, Moses Conegliano, who sold it to a Christian in 1840. But after other transfers of ownership during a robust real estate market, in 1858 it was purchased by the wealthy Errera brothers, bankers, after a series of moves in the vicinity that started in 1811. Major, though controversial, renovations were carried out in 1865. Several families went to live there (Abramo and his wife Enrichetta Jacur, and those of his sons Beniamino, a landowner and shopkeeper, and Mosè Vita, a banker). With them came three maids, all Jewish, as well as some from the Trieste and Ravà families. In the Austrian Land Registry (1841) thirteen units were counted under the name of the Errera brothers' company just in Cannaregio and they included homes and part of the courtyard in Rio Tera Due Ponti and calle Caliari, shops on the fondamenta Ormesini, two warehouses on the ground floor in calle del Cristo and the home located in calle Ca' d'Oro. It was a very significant capital increase from what appeared in the 1771 land registry when only Abram Errera rented a house owned by Lorenzo Grimani, paying fifty-two ducats of rent. We know nothing of the family in 1805. But already in 1811, his father Beniamino, who was then fifty-three years old, left the ghetto, going to live not far away, in the contrada of San Geremia; after that date, the family moved often, staying in the vicinity (in 1848, 1851, 1858, 1859, 1860, and 1863), always in houses that they owned. In their march forward, they also settled for some time in calle Ca' d'Oro, in a building, which might not have been very prestigious, since the census annuity was only 42,24 lire, located next to the palazzo.[6] The Errera would live in the palazzo for thirty-six years. As of 1894, the pres-

6. Calabi, "Gli ebrei veneziani," 164–65.

tigious medieval building, although sold by the well-known bankers, remained in Jewish hands. Giorgio Franchetti, a member of another family of bankers, this time originally from Mantua, and in turn a collector of works of fifteenth and sixteenth century art, bought it at a relatively low price because of its poor condition and internal division in many apartments. Restoration was begun, but never completed, and Franchetti then donated to the Italian state in 1916, still however personally supervising the restoration based on the remaining parts of the building that were found and identical remake of the missing pieces (including the marble paving on the ground floor, inspired by that of the basilica San Marco). The Museum, which, along with the Franchetti collection, holds other works acquired in the meantime, was inaugurated in 1927.

In 1810, the majestic palace not far away, built in the early seventeenth century by the Fontana in San Felice, on the Grand Canal, was purchased by German banker Giovanni Corrado Reck—who rented several apartments—but the building did not remain in his hands very long. In 1845, Giuseppe Finzi, son of Aron, bought the property and then resold it to Giacomo Ventura in 1856. The property changed hands again in 1862, when it was acquired by the banking company of Jacob Levi, represented by his son Angelo, who remained the only owner for about twenty years. Angelo settled in the apartment on the main floor with his wife, his children, his grandmother Enrichetta, two grandchildren and the servants. The third floor of the building remained vacant for a long time. Since then, ownership has remained in the family, and the palazzo was inherited by the Sullams, with whom the Levi family became related.[7]

---

7. Calabi, "Gli ebrei veneziani," 165–68.

But who were these Levis, able to make a real estate purchase of such importance shortly after the middle of the century just three years after the operation by the Erreras? As early as 1805, they were residing nearby, in calle Polli: three families (of Venetian origin, plebeian and shopkeepers all), a total of thirteen people. We do not know when they arrived in the city, but they definitely were among the first Venetian Jews to make the choice of "leaving" the ghetto, where they still had a house in 1771, in sacca delle Muneghe, and a shop near the San Girolamo canal. Their business must have thrived, since they moved progressively from the commercial to the banking sector; some of them, if not the whole family, were engaged in international trade.

In 1850, it was a grandson of Mandolin, Abramo Levi son of Giacomo with his wife and children who moved to Palazzo Fontana. In 1857, his brother Angelo joined him in the same house, after an intermediate move nearby in 1851.

Less than thirty years later, in 1881, Cavaliere Giacomo Levi (son of Angelo) after a long stay in the palace of San Felice with his father and brothers, moved into one of the most prestigious places in the city, the Procuratie Vecchie. The family possessions had become considerable in the meantime and included fourteen houses, seven warehouses, four workshops, vegetable gardens, a garden, a part of an abandoned road and other fragments of land (in addition to the listings on the land registry map mentioned above) recorded in the census district of Cannaregio. They also owned five houses, a shop and some storerooms in Castello, two houses with courtyards in San Polo and San Marco. In addition, they had a great deal of property in other towns, especially in the province of Treviso (where there was for example a country home).

Then, in 1881, the building was given to Giacomo, who transferred it to his sister Giovannina, wife of Benedetto Sullam seven years later (1888). The size of the building was such that, beyond the owner, it housed various branches of the family as well as servants, often Catholic.

But Benedetto Sullam—who became owner of Palazzo Fontana towards the end of the century thanks to marriage—and the gradual growth of the family wealth is worth studying. In this case, the purchase of real estate was more fragmented, though the family insisted on residing in Cannaregio. In the 1771 Venetian land registry, Benedetto Sullam figured as a tenant of certain properties, including a workshop in Ghetto Vecchio although the Sullams not appear certain among families of higher social status in the Mortera registry. Benedetto, "shopkeeper" aged fifty-five, from San Daniele del Friuli, had seven children. He lived in a modest dwelling (which he bought a few years later) on the sixth and seventh floor of presumably one of most dilapidated buildings in Ghetto Vecchio, one of two at "Scala Matta", where he had only one servant.

However, with the funds accumulated, he soon managed to buy nine houses and a shop. When in 1801 the Treves-Bonfil and Vivante together paid nearly third of the 1,200 carats that made up the tribute to the Università degli Ebrei of 135 families then registered for tax purposes, Benedict (despite being thirtieth on the list) was only taxed 6 carats, 0.5% of the total. In short, he was wealthy, but certainly not among the richest. Yet in 1808 the family already had fifty apartments in the city (many of them in Cannaregio, but also in the districts of San Cancian, Santissimi Apostoli, Santa Croce, San Giovanni in Bragora, San Geminiano, San Giacomo di Rialto, San Maria Mater Domini and even in Torcello—in other words scattered everywhere—and a number of shops acquired very quickly. On the other hand, after 1809, the pace of city purchases apparently decreased, in keeping with increased agriculture interests on the mainland.[8]

8. Antonio Lazzarini, *Fra terra e acqua. L'azienda risicola di una famiglia veneziana nel delta del Po*, Rome: Edizioni di Storia e Letteratura 1995.

Ultimately, towards the middle of the century, using the Austro-Italian land register as a source, there is a sort of "Jewish island" in the immediate vicinity of Palazzo Fontana and Ca' d'Oro when a number of real estate transactions of varying dimensions took place within fifty years. Looking further, it is clear that good number of those who left the ghetto in the period between the first few years of freedom and the 1820s initially seemed to have moved a few hundred meters, remaining in the same *sestiere*. Presumably they used the same community facilities, including the urban structures they were used to, probably willing to move again and again, according to their growing families or the desire for better housing.

Towards the end of the century, however, a large number of Jews resided in other *sestieri* and probably included all income groups. Even the Chief Rabbi, Moses Coen Porto (who officiated at the Spanish School) lived in the Maddalena area; as he walked to synagogue, his stately garb and demeanor aroused the curiosity of passersby.[9]

SCATTERED THROUGHOUT THE CITY

In the second half of the century, many Jews in all income groups abandoned the ghetto. Along with the Levi acquisition of the Procuratie Vecchie,[10] the purchase of three other buildings of great value in San Marco marked the process of assimilation (the seventeenth century Palazzo Barozzi, whose main façade faces the Rio di San Moise at the corner of the Grand Canal; the palazzo in calle San Benedetto facing the rio di San Luca, not far from where it empties into the Grand

---

9. Emilio Pardo, *Luci ed ombre*, Venice: self published 1965, 17.

10. Martina Massaro, "Gli investimenti ebraici a Venezia al principio del XIX secolo: il ruolo dei Treves e l'acquisto della procuratia a San Marco," *Venetica* ser. 3, 2 (2016), 7–28.

Canal, and San Vidal). They were bought a few years later by other well-to-do Jews, sometimes also great collectors and patrons of famous architects (the Treves, the Bonfil, the Cavalieri, the Ravenna, and the Franchetti).[11]

Of all of them, the case of Giacomo Treves is of particular significance from the point of view of inclusion in the Venetian society. For Treves, philanthropy was a determining factor of the family's culture and policy, along with a large-scale economic program (land acquisition and reclamation in the eastern Veneto region and in the southern Verona region). He showed a keen interest both in associations in the agricultural sector, and the fine arts, and with his brother Isacco he was involved in the humanities, the arts, botany and garden art, music and theater. Significantly, he was directly engaged in institutions in and outside Venice (the Academy of Fine Arts, the Chamber of Commerce, the Ateneo Veneto, the City Council, the Cassa di Risparmio, and the Botanical Garden of Padua) where he held important offices. In this framework of activities on several fronts, the choice in 1827 to buy Palazzo Barozzi on the Grand Canal in the parish of San Moise, the nerve center of business, merely sealed the two Treves brothers' assimilation in the city. In their hands, the building was completely re-modernized and decorated in stages, with the guidance of art and architecture expert Leopoldo Cicognara. The purchase of two giant statues by Antonio Canova, *Hector* and *Ajax*, finalized the restoration of the building, redesigned as museum to house an important collection of works of "modern" art that the Treves were assembling (fig. 22). Giuseppe Borsato, an academic, artist, and decorator then engaged redecorating the Royal Palace in Piazza San Marco, as well as in the Villa Pisani at Stra and the theater La Fenice as well as the

---

11. Massaro, "Gli investimenti ebraici a Venezia," 25.

restoration for major Venetian families was entrusted with designing the room for the two sculptures. Apsidal, double height, with central trabeation supported by two Ionic columns and three windows framing the Punta della Dogana, the focus of the building welcomed and emphasized Canova's two giants with light. The revamping of other rooms by Giovanni de Min, an artist from Belluno who the Treves brothers commissioned in the fall of 1829, again on the advice of Cicognara, was interrupted. Inside the building, they carried out financial and business affairs, as well as hosting balls that even attracted distinguished guests from Vienna. But the social and cultural environment where the family moved was still one of fashionable artists (Francesco Hayez, Ippolito Caffi, Sebastiano Santi) and Milanese salons frequented by leading musicians of the period (Bellini, Donizetti, Pacini, and Gioachino Rossini),[12] again emphasizing—if needed—the role now assumed by the family in the city.

And finally, Palazzo Franchetti in San Vidal received particularly attention in the local press: Baron Raimondo Franchetti (from the same family that purchased Ca' d'Oro after Errera), new owner of the building (figs. 23–24), around 1883 engaged a particularly "innovative architect", Camillo Boito (although we know that in this case he collaborated with others, engineer Alessandro Manetti and decorator Carlo Matscheg). From an assimilated Jewish family—to the point of being styled "Baron"—Raimondo was a significant character in the history of Italian exploration and colonialism, showing exceptional passion for the esoteric. The new owner's needs were particularly recognizable in what Boito himself considered a clear and visible "addition" to the building: the wide monumental staircase as vertical connection of the three floors, a

---

12. Martina Massaro, *Giacomo Treves de Bonfil, collezionista e mecenate*, Ph.D. thesis, Scuola dottorale inter-ateneo in "Storia delle Arti," Venice 2014.

modification of the building that had already been redesigned by Giovan Battista Meduna not many years before.

Ultimately, some of these owners, coming from outside the city with wealth accumulated elsewhere, entered a vibrant and sound real estate market. The tendency to move further from Cannaregio was a second stage of the Venetian Jews' economic growth: in thirty years, a group of bankers already rich in the late eighteenth century came to concentrate an immense capital in their hands and use it in part to redevelop an extensive portfolio of property reduced to a state of complete ruin.

However, even apart from striking cases examined, in the second half of the nineteenth century, the Jewish population was spread throughout the city, albeit with a tendency to group together. In 1869, seventy-two percent of the Jews living in Cannaregio, twenty-three percent in San Marco, and four percent in Castello, were often grouped by civil registry numbers;[13] in 1911 they spread out even further, albeit still affiliated to their family, neighbors and class.[14]

A NEW GENERATION OF ENTREPRENEURS

Even before the fall of the Republic, the business of some bankers and merchants had moved in a strong international direction. The dealings of the House of Daniel Bonfil and son with Marseilles and Constantinople in the years between 1773 and 1794 are a good demonstration.[15] The entrepre-

---

13. *Rilievo degli abitanti di Venezia 1869 per religione, condizioni, professioni, arti e mestieri*, Venice: Antonelli 1875, 125.

14. Comune di Venezia, *Relazione sul V Censimento demografico*, Venice: Officine grafiche Carlo Ferrari 1912, 142–43; Sergio Della Pergola, *Anatomia dell'ebraismo italiano*, Rome-Assisi: Carucci 1976, 74.

15. Giovanni Levi, "I commerci della Casa Daniele Bonfil e figlio con Marsiglia e Costantinopoli (1773–1794)," in Stefano Gasparri, Giovanni Levi, Pierandrea Moro, (eds.), *Venezia. Itinerari per la storia della città*, Bologna: Il Mulino 1997, 223–43.

neurial activity of some Venetian Jews after the arrival of the French was entirely consistent with real estate and land investments in the second half of the nineteenth century.

Proving to be an effective businessman, like his father Iseppo (the same who had acquired the palazzo of San Moise and was related to the Bonfils) who purchased state property offered for sale by Napoleon in 1811, Giacomo Treves and his brother initially shared ownership of vessels, merchandise, jewelry, silverware.[16] Then, starting in 1830, along with his rich collection of works of art, he worked to obtain the granting of free port in Venice from the Emperor Franz of Austria, (1806–1835).[17] We know from Cicognara that great results from the new authorization were generally expected, thanks to the arrival of foreigners in the city ready to invest in different sectors. For Treves de Bonfil that meant political and financial commitments, obviously aimed at strengthening the image of his bank and trading company, but also to create international and cosmopolitan economy after the fall of the Venetian Republic.[18] And indeed, the years of the 1840s were a kind of Renaissance: to accompany the free port, the greatest exponents of the Chamber of Commerce—Reali, Papadopoli and Treves himself—also created an integrated infrastructure network, including the Malamocco dam, completion of the Murazzi (seawalls at the Lido), the new railway Venice-Milan with the trans-lagoon bridge, and the

---

16. Martina Massaro, "Giacomo Treves de' Bonfili (1788-1885) collezionista e imprenditore," in Xavier Barral i Altet e Michele Gottardi, (eds.), *La storia dell'arte a Venezia ieri e oggi: duecento anni di studi*, Venice: 2013 (=*Ateneo Veneto* ser. 12/I, no. 3).

17. Giovanni Tommasoni, "Porto Franco, Industria e Commercio," in *Venezia e le sue lagune*, Vol. 2, Venice: Antonelli 1847, 526; Emilio Morpurgo, *Saggi statistici ed economici sul Veneto*, Padua: Prosperini 1868, 297–300, 328–29, 333–39; Alberto Errera, *Storia e statistica delle industrie venete e accenni al loro avvenire*, Venice: Antonelli 1870, 743–753.

18. Massaro,"Giacomo Treves,"258–59.

river network. The enthusiasm and vitality of these figures, exponents of a new Venetian leadership, signaled a phase of "continued prosperity, growing, vibrant ... as to seem miraculous" - as careful observer, though closely linked to the family, Agostino Sagredo argued in contemporary article.[19]

Jews were members of the Board of Directors of Società Veneta di Navigazione Lagunare (the Venetian Lagoon Navigation Society, 1873), and others who were involved in regular trade between Venice and Calcutta.

Particularly significant, and also affected by the Jewish presence, was the breath of Europeanism that swept over the island of Giudecca with the participation of foreign companies in what was once primarily local production: a mingling of nationalities and technical innovation changed urban reality, as old activities were expanded and new ones created.[20] The Supervisory Committee of the Privileged Arts of the Enclosure of the Free Port of Venice, established December 12, 1829 on acceptance of the Austrian Government, carried out controls, offering companies a range of reliefs from customs excesses against Austria even when it withdrew from the Veneto region. It was active at least until 1878 and is still a source of valuable information. The most flourishing industries on the island were those related to the production of ropes and leather followed by furnaces, and production of cream of tartar for food and wax. Between 1833 and 1844, particularly intense activity boasted of dynamic actors in both the local and Jewish populations. Among the flourishing leather goods production, for example, one of the most important was that

---

19. Agostino Sagredo, *Notizie sugli ammiglioramenti di Venezia* (extract from *Annali Universali di Statistica*, July 1843, 6; January-February, 1844, 4).

20. Anna Di Giovanni, *Giudecca Ottocento. Le trasformazioni di un'isola nella prima età industriale*, Venice, Istituto Veneto di Scienze, Lettere ed Arti 2009.

owned by Samuele Moravia,[21] with a slow transformation from small craft to a more advanced technological development. With other companies, Moravia's effectively contributed to the progressive decline of some smaller companies on the island. In 1835, for instance, he hired the workers of the competing leatherworks owned by fellow Jew Giuseppe Gerlin, and then in 1853 acquired the entire workshop from Angela Saoner, Gerlin's wife. Even the Levi bankers mentioned earlier entered the market, buying the properties owned by Saoner-Gerlin and Bernarda Gerlin respectively in 1861 and in 1873, only to turn them into warehouses and shops of various kinds (as shown in the Austro-Italian land registry).

Instead, Salomon Rothschild imported steam machines to make cream of tartar, making the horse powered Weber grinding tartar company noncompetitive.[22] Starting in 1847, Rothschild became aware of the change of scale that made Venice the center of gravity between Austria and the Adriatic and of the bitumen quarries of Dalmatia and Istria and therefore industrial outpost for the Milan-Venice railway line. As a result, Rothschild set up the first asphalt factory there with as many as 45 employees.[23]

In addition, between 1844 and 1857, with great entrepreneurial skill, Salomon Rothschild formed a partnership with the French entrepreneur Charles Astruc. Attempting to revive an ancient lagoon production that had virtually disappeared—salt—the businessmen set up a company in the northeastern area, in Motta di San Felice between Burano

---

21. ASV, *Commissione sorveglianza alle fabbriche del portofranco,* 1833–1835, b. 15, fol. 7; 1838–1844, b. 22, fol. 4; 1845–1872, b. 51, fol. 8.

22. ASV, *Commissione sorveglianza alle fabbriche del portofranco,* 1845–1849, b. 52, fol. 3.

23. ASV, *Camera di Commercio,* b. 176, III, 4, no. 1285, February 1847; Adolfo Bernardello, "Venezia 1830-1866. Iniziative economiche, accumulazione e investimenti di capitale," *Il Risorgimento,* 1 (2002): 5–66.

and Torcello, for the extraction, exploitation and commer-
cialization of new salt.[24] They built offices, warehouses and
accommodations on the island, and the system remained in
operation until 1913.

Towards the end of the century, following in the steps of
the great banker born in Frankfurt, but of Austrian citizenship, other international capitalists (such as Junghans, Her-
ion, Stucky, Neville) or closer to the political powers (like
Volpi, or Papadopoli) were called to Venice. These leaders
proposed a comprehensive framework of investment and
were the *de facto* architects of Venice's industrial modernization. The panorama certainly changed, especially in the
second half of the century, partly at the expense of the old
workshops.

Other business activities strongly characterized Venetian
development of the first decades of the twentieth century,
where the Jewish presence was far from secondary. The birth
of the Italian Company of Grand Hotels, the basis of the Lido's success as a seaside resort was directed by Baron Alberto
Treves de Bonfil, chairman of the Board of Directors (on
which Paul Errera also sat).[25]

In the context that concerns us here, the Jewish history of
civic engagement in the establishment of the lagoon hospital, the seaside establishments and the first great hotels at the
Lido has yet to be written.[26]

---

24. Giovanni Tommasoni, *Della salina di S. Felice nella lagune di Venezia. Indicazioni,* Milan: Società degli editori degli Annali universali delle scienze e dell'industria 1854; *Plan de la saline S. felice fondée par M.
Le Baron S. M. de Rotschild et Charles Astruc dans la lagune de Venise,*
Venice: Lith. Ripamonti Carpano 1857.

25. Paolo Gerbaldo, *Compagnia italiana dei grandi alberghi. Un sogno
italiano dalla Belle Epoque al Miracolo economico (1906-1979),* Turin:
Giappichelli 2015.

26. Nelli Vanzan Marchini, (ed.), *Venezia e il suo Ospedale dal XVI al
XX secolo,* Venice: Arsenale 1999, 65–80.

THE TWENTIETH CENTURY: INTEGRATION

A century after the decree granting them freedom, Venetian Jews (the 1901 census recorded a Jewish population of 2,474) were substantially integrated into society and the urban fabric: some fully involved in the city's political, cultural and economic elite. Overall, the Risorgimento and the Great War were moments that built Italy and the Jews—often close to Daniele Manin, whose Jewish origins were known, and who was considered by all father of the Venetian homeland—participated, not without contradictions and tensions, in Venetian patriotism.[27]

In the first decades of the twentieth century, the presence of the Jewish bourgeoisie in Venetian society became quite substantial. Although part of the same network, built on meetings and consolidated family relationships, the group was varied in terms of social position, attitudes, ideas, and relationship with religious traditions.[28] The birth of a Venetian Zionist movement dated back to 1903; its members included younger and older professionals, well-known in the city and generally very attached to the Jewish community. And yet they did not necessarily share the same ideals: some (such as lawyers Raffaello Levi and Alberto Musatti) became part of nationalist circles and were members of the Ca' Pesaro Association (promoting modern arts and culture). The war in Libya and the First World War accentuated patriotic loyalty; and then there were those who joined the Venetian mayor Riccardo Selvatico's progressive government and those who supported clerical-moderate mayor Filippo Grimani. In short, participation in public and administrative life, which intensified with the unification of the Veneto

---

27. Simon Levis Sullam, *Una comunità immaginata. Gli ebrei a Venezia 1900-1938*, Milan: Unicopli 2001, 241–48.

28. Sullam, *Una comunità immaginata*, 10.

to the Kingdom of Italy, understandably did not have only one political connotation. National well-known personalities such as psychoanalyst Cesare Musatti, or Cesare and Margherita Sarfatti were among the founders of the socialist weekly *Il Secolo Nuovo*, but then some adhered passionately to Fascism, like the famous patron of the Novecento group of artists, Margherita Sarfatti, who later had an affair with Mussolini. The economic historian Gino Luzzatto, a professor and then rector of Ca' Foscari University, follower of Marc Bloch, Henri Pirenne and the *Annales* School, was among the pioneers of the "Manifesto of the Anti-Fascist Intellectuals of Benedetto Croce", while engineer Angelo Fano, also an anti-fascist militant and later a member of the movement Giustizia e Libertà (Justice and Freedom) remained a member of the Republican Party until emigrating to Palestine. Finally, the bank lawyer Max Ravà (his father Graziano belonged to the Liberal party) joined the association of young Monarchists.

In 1932 the community board approved the creation of a Jewish primary school in the ghetto, but actually only less than half of Jewish children (those from poorer families) attended. Moreover, aware that his co-religionists resided all over the city, Rabbi Ottolenghi complained of being unable to open the school in a more central area and felt compelled to mention that the new school was for everyone, "regardless of social class" and was not to be considered "a charity, not a cultural institution." And for higher levels of education, there was no doubt that wealthy Jews were attending public high schools[29] throughout the Fascist period until the racial laws were enacted.

---

29. Sullam, *Una comunità immaginata*, 118–19.

... AND DISINTEGRATION

Starting in 1935, the Ministry of the Interior subjected the community of Venice (like most in Italy) to the supervision of a commissioner (Aldo Coen Porto until 1937, then Aldo Finzi).

Following a telegram from that Ministry on August 11, 1938, Venice, like other Italian cities, was required to distribute instructions for the prefect and surveyors with forms for the census of the population "of Jewish race even if professing another, or no religion." At the end of the month, and based on this survey, the city declared the presence of 2136 people, including 1471 of the Jewish religion, 616 Catholics and 49 agnostics.[30] On that date, a remarkable number were still living in Cannaregio, but there was a considerable presence in San Marco, where many professionals were located. The Civil Registry showed that, of those 2136, 158 were shop-owners, 164 office workers, and 103 were wealthy (i.e. living off private incomes). There were thirty-four professors and teachers, thirty-one lawyers, twenty-three engineers, and seventeen doctors. In September Benito Mussolini stated. "It is time for Italians proclaim themselves racist." In those same days people began posting signs on the shutters of the shops owned by Jews and decidedly anti-Semitic articles were published in the local press. On the 15th of the month, the chief of police notified Rome of the dismissal of Jewish executives of Assicurazioni Generali and that "others occupying important posts" were to be let go. Few of those fired were young but on September 5, Jewish youth were excluded from public schools (middle and secondary school diplomas noted the students' "race"). The decree of September 23, 1938 al-

---

30. Renata Segre, (ed.), *Gli ebrei a Venezia 1938-1945. Una comunità tra persecuzione e rinascita*, Venice: Il Cardo 1995.

lowed elementary school education for fifty-six children in Cannaregio (the number grew to seventy in 1939) and two teachers. A provisional middle school course was organized in calle del Remedio and then transferred to Ponte Stor-to at San Filippo e Giacomo; there was talk of "technical studies, useful for engaging young people in the only career choices still accessible, those of small business, small indus-try and handicraft and—hopefully—agriculture." On Jan-uary 5, 1939, a recognized Jewish middle school equalized with a classical lyceum and a lower technical school were authorized at Ponte Storto. The school made adjustments to welcome students from other secondary programs (teaching and scientific) for a total of fifty-two students.

The community's welfare activities, such as a summer camp at the Lido, the charitable work of the ADEI (Association of Italian Jewish Women), the rest home for the elderly, and a soup kitchen for the poor and for transit Jews, continued but on a reduced basis.

The decree law of February 9, 1939 set limits to property ownership of the Jews, prohibiting transfer free of charge and mortgages.

Few seem to dispute these bans: contemporary police information only reported the incident of a priest in the Church of San Silvestro who "said phrases such as to merit a hard lesson that unfortunately has not been imposed"[31] and instead emphasized the continued presence of Venetian Jews in the professions (doctors and lawyers in particular). But in June of the following year (1939) the Fascist unions (which substituted professional associations) implemented restric-tive measures, so that in 1940 a memorandum spread the list of members deleted from the rosters, who were therefore prohibited from practicing their professions.

---

31. Segre, *Gli ebrei a Venezia*, 56.

July 25, 1943, date of the fall of fascism, did not mean immediate improvement for the circumstances of the Venetian Jews. Indeed, two months later, the president of the community, Giuseppe Jona committed suicide to avoid having to hand over a list of his co-religionists to the German authorities who in November were still working to reconstruct the birth, marriage and repudiation of Judaism records to begin deportation.[32] This happened in December 1943, with detainees sent to the Carpi concentration camp and then to Auschwitz the following February. A simulacrum of Jewish life in the ghetto continued during the eighteen-month Nazi-Fascist persecution, especially around the Shelter House and the nearby elementary school. However, between 1944 and the early months of 1945, the number of deportees doubled as they were hunted in and around the city (the countryside, religious institutions), with roundups even among the elderly and the hospitalized. At the time of the Liberation on April 25, the number of the deported reached 230.

The turning point for reconstruction came on May 11, when a community revival project was presented. The community's board was reconstituted June 24. During those months, the prefect ordered restitution of all the rights of Italian and foreign Jews. The return to normalcy was not sudden however as anti-Semitic phrases were gradually erased from the street, displaced persons removed from Jewish homes, Jews resumed their jobs, the three synagogues (Spanish, Levantine and Canton) were reopened, and Jewish cultural, recreational, political and welfare to young people and women associations began to meet again in the Montefiore community center. In June 1945, the ritual objects and silverware that had been hidden under the *aron* of the Canton School were retrieved.

---

32. Venice, Istituto Veneto di Scienze, Lettere ed Arti, seminar on Giuseppe Jona, 14 November 2013.

Community life resumed albeit slowly, with growing participation; and yet, the disrupture in Jewish life, not only in Venice, but in all of Europe, can never be forgotten.

TRAVELERS' GLIMPSE OF THE GHETTO

While this is far from being a systematic study on a subject of great interest, it is worth remembering that—in effective short strokes and immediate images—travelers' descriptions confirm what archives narrate more systematically. On the other hand, guides to the city paid little attention to the ghetto (the guide republished several times by Giulio Lorenzetti devoted only a few lines to it), while, on the other, a foreigner rarely left Venice without visiting the ghetto. Travelers wrote particularly vibrant notes, intrigued by the wealth of events that took place, amazed and fascinated by customs so different from those they knew—religious ceremonies, festivals, theater, music, and funerals, at times seasoned with a hint of anti-Jewish feeling. Sometimes their observations were based on a long series of platitudes, celebrating the welcome they extended to foreign Venetians, or their "pleasure" in watching the most diverse rituals.

Not many years after the ghetto was established, Marc'Antonio Muret—particularly grateful to the Republic for the teaching position obtained in San Francesco della Vigna—insisted with emphatic oratory on safety even for those who arrived in the city at night. Anyone could circulate in tranquility, save the Moors with dark faces and those with tight curls in their hair, those who lived along the shores of the Gange or who came from the shores of Tanai. Still, he could not avoid comments, adopted by many, regarding frauds and dishonorable earnings engaged in by "Jewish people."[1]

---

1. Marc'Antoine Muret, *Opera* (1555), in Jacopo Morelli, *Componimenti poetici di vari autori in lode di Venezia*, Venice: Albrizzi 1792, 91.

In 1611, the Englishman Thomas Coryat described his amazed impressions. Though he provided inflated figures about the number of inhabitants (between five and six thousand), he immediately grasped the intermingling of communities with very different in origins and customs (those born in Western countries used a red headdress; the Orientals, those of Jerusalem, Alexandria, Constantinople adopted turbans, as did the Turks). He was particularly struck by the seven synagogues, as a place of community meeting of all (men, women, children), their internal spatial organization, their bright illumination (an enormous number of candlesticks were lit during ceremonies). He observed the swaying movements of those who read the sacred texts, the irreverence of people attending services (who, upon entering, did not uncover their heads, or genuflect, or perform any other act of submission to God), the separation between men and women (often beautiful and bejeweled like English countesses, sitting in their gallery above). Coryat was amazed by the "sober, distinct and orderly" reading during the religious service, but that he often found too loud, like the recitation of psalms that sounded like an incomprehensible "bleating". He felt the need to give some indirect information about a people that intrigued him and were far from a marginal presence in Venice: Jews do not use images; they are so respectful of their "sabbath" that they do not buy, not sell, nor do anything profane or secular on that day; circumcision (which unfortunately he was unable to attend) was a health care, as well as a religious practice, done "with a stone knife" to boys on the eighth day after birth.

The most arresting part of the story, however, was his own firsthand experience: after walking a long time in the campo di Ghetto Nuovo to look around, by chance he met there a learned rabbi, with deep knowledge of Latin (some have speculated it

might have been Leon Modena),[2] with whom he struck up a learned discussion on the divinity of Christ. But the pleasant tour
and lively theological conversation degenerated into a scuffle,
over the reaction of at least 40-50 people who suddenly appeared from every corner of the square, offended because he dared
to criticize their religion. It was only thanks to his country's ambassador that he managed to get out, rescued at the last minute
by his noble secretary. The ambassador and his secretary were
passing on a gondola under the bridge of the Ormesini, just as
the Englishman was trying to get away from an enclosure that
suddenly seemed too dense and dangerous. Coryat recounted
the event with a mixture of astonishment and irritation, attracted and fascinated by the diversity, interested in the life of
a particular, crowded neighborhood where an educated debate
can take place in the street. His description clearly outlined the
role (protection for some and threatening for others) that the
space, the island surrounded by the canal, and the importance
that the "existence of mandated access" had for those inside.[3]

Even the Duke of Orleans asked to be conducted to the ghetto
in 1629 and walked there, accompanied by his following. And
only a few decades later, the Secretary of the Embassy of France, Alexandre Toussaint Limojon de Saint Didier, seemed fascinated by the beautiful wedding parties: alongside magnificent-
ly dressed Jewish guests there were Venetian ladies, masked to
avoid being recognized. Much admired is the story of the marriage of a daughter of the wealthy Levi dal Banco with many
guests and even the presence of several foreign ministers.[4]

2. Elena Rossi Artom, Umberto Fortis, Ariel Viterbo, (eds.), *Vita di Je-
hudà, Autobiografia di Leon Modena, rabbino veneziano del XVII secolo*,
Turin: Zamorani 2000.

3. Thomas Coryat, *Coryat's crudities*, London: William Stansby 1611
(reprinted London 1776), Vol. 1, 296–304.

4. Cited in Jean Georgelin, *Venise au siècle des lumières*, Paris: Walter de
Gruyter 1978, 676, 944.

Toussaint de Saint Didier, secretary and trusted adviser of the ambassador of Louis XIV in the Republic, held what became a common opinion: there was no place in Italy where the Jews were treated better than in Venice. In his description of 1680, after accompanying the diplomat of Avaux through the ghetto of Venice, he noted that on one hand terrain was so scarce that extraordinary building density was necessary, on the other hand the proverbial tolerance of the Venetians was such that every noble house counted some fond friends of absolute trust among the Jews. The aristocrats, seeing their friends' discretion, became protectors and, at the same time, used them for more than one purpose. To de Saint Didier, the Venetian Jews appeared not "tolerated" but "associated" in the richest trade routes in the Levant, attracting large sums of money, as well as contributing to the state budget with regular and special taxes. In the eyes of foreigners, they were distinguished from the rest of the Christians only because they wore a stylish hat of the finest scarlet cloth ever seen, lined with shiny black taffeta.[5]

The Lido cemetery also attracted travelers' attention: its decadence in the eighteenth and nineteenth century was effectively evoked by famous writers in more or less famous testimony of their trips to Venice.

In October 1786, Wolfgang Goethe related that the tombs of two contiguous, Jewish and Anglican, areas at the extremity of the island were concealed by the sand piled up by the wind.[6] In 1816 British consul Hoppner, telling of his ri-

5. ANP, *Affaires Etrangères*, b. 1, 1162, 31 August 1709; Alexandre Toussaint Limojon de Saint Didier, *La ville et la Republique de Venise*, Paris: 1680, Vol. 1, 172; *Relazione della città e Repubblica di Venezia*, 1672, 30–32.

6. Carla Boccato, *L'antico cimitero di San Nicolò di Lido a Venezia*, Venice: Comitato per il centro storico ebraico di Venezia, 1980, 5, 14, note 17: the Anglican cemetery had been opened near the old fort of San Nicolò circa 1684.

des along the beach with his friend Lord Byron, recalled the place, now clearly accessible to all, "where the French had broken down the enclosure and /dug up the grave stones". Two years later, in the preface of his "Julian and Maddalo", Shelley, also riding at the Lido in the company of Byron, uses images of uncultivated and abandoned land to describe the same strip.

In 1834, after a quarrel with George Sand, Alfred de Musset evoked his beloved jumping "from tomb to tomb" in anger, while Theophile Gauthier recalled the abandonment of an area where children could play among broken tombstones.[7]

7. Boccato, *L'antico cimitero di San Nicolò*, 5–6.

GHETTOS TODAY

Salvatore Settis, referring to Richard Sennett, argues that "the experience of the Jews in the Venetian ghetto was a way of linking culture and political rights that could last over time". In what was then the "most cosmopolitan city in Europe", or rather "the first global city of the modern world", the ghetto community was able to develop that "sense of mutual solidarity" and "forms of collective representation", focusing on an awareness of their rights which made the Venetian enclosure the general emblem of a place where "freedom of speech tended to coincide with the right to the city."[1]

Current ghettos are perceived as dangerous places, conditioned by economic insecurity, a high rate of immigration and, despite this, a potential cosmopolitanism with the chance for people from different backgrounds to meet, share experiences and co-exist.

The word "ghetto" is commonly used in the media today to define very different situations from a social and geopolitical viewpoint. Louis Wirth played an important role in spreading this expression. Probably without knowing the fifteenth century manuscripts found by Tomaso Temanza in the second half of the eighteenth century when he drafted his scholarly comment to the earliest cartographic representation image of Venice,[2] but perhaps knowing Venetian historiography through indirect sources, the American sociologist spoke of

---

1. Richard Sennett, *The Foreiner*, London: Notting Hill Editions, 2011; Salvatore Settis, *Se Venezia muore*, Turin: Einaudi 2014, 144–45.

2. Tommaso Temanza, *Antica pianta dell'inclita città di Venezia* [...], Venice: Stamperia di Carlo Palese 1781, 70–72.

this institution as a case of prolonged social isolation within a city. He did not limit himself to the Jewish question, but on the contrary widened his considerations to other episodes of segregation with a functional goal, stating that it was one of the so-called natural areas of the city ... affecting both those who lived within, and outside its walls.[3]

With these statements he triggered the term's use to describe to a closed supervised city space with restricted movement for minorities involuntarily living and working there. Before that, in the early twentieth century, Emilio Teza, a Venetian writer, raised the issue, but his contribution enjoyed a mostly local audience.[4] Later, the term "ghetto" was the subject of numerous studies by other sociologists, Italian, American, and Israeli Jewish scholars, some of whom were experts on Venice and some not.[5] But the topic is still the subject of reflection and comparative studies of today's multiple realities in different geographical contexts, without forgetting the original intentions to separate groups of the population, without entirely removing them from the urban context.[6]

It should be emphasized that at least since the fifteenth century, with the many archival references to the copper smelter, in some contemporary documents the word *geto* also meant taxation, in particular on the work of excavation of canals and maintenance of canal banks, bridges, and wells. In 1425, for example, at a time of overt urban decay, the Maggior Consiglio ordered the collection in all districts of a *geto* and again, in 1458, home owners were taxed considerably by

---

3. Louis Wirth, *The Ghetto*, Chicago: Chicago University Press [1928].

4. E. Teza, "Intorno alla voce Ghetto. Dubbi da togliere e da risvegliare," Atti del Regio Istituto Veneto di Scienze, Lettere ed Arti 63 (1903–1904): 1273–86.

5. For a selected bibliography, see Concina, "Parva Jerusalem," 46n2.

6. Mitchell Duneier, *Ghetto: The Invention of a Place, the History of an Idea*, New York: Farrar, Straus and Giroux 2016.

the Piovego and the *Capi dei Sestieri* "in accordance with custom", while in 1460 the Giudici del Piovego went on daily rounds to ensure that "those responsible" would pay the *geto* to allow cleaning of the canals and maintenance of bridges, wells and roads.[7] Perhaps the two expressions both ended up identifying the obligation for the area inhabitants to pay taxes to the Republic.

It is difficult to say how much the anomaly of the site and its location in a peripheral area devoid of large buildings played in creating the definition *par excellence* a place of segregation. For Wirth, one trait that qualified it was the residence of "foreigners" (medieval Europeans' awareness of the presence of foreigners within their communities is common knowledge). The other was the issue of a formal decree of the state that distinguished this case from the many episodes of voluntary aggregation, corresponding to practices rooted in religious customs and habits. But Wirth notes that while neither of these traits was unique, they were tested together in the lagoon city.

And this realization goes beyond the slightly abstract considerations of urban planners of the last decades of the nineteenth century (Camillo Sitte, Joseph Stübben, John Ruskin), who insisted on the morphological closing of space to induce a perception of security, and therefore on the importance of the discipline of the eye: that guide to looking proposed more recently by American scholars of public spaces who stress that the closed form of the square suggests a particular atmosphere.[8] In particular, aside from the legally decreed conditions and constraints, the real city was something different

7. ASV, *Maggior Consiglio*, Deliberazioni, 22 April 1425, Reg. 22 (Ursa), fol. 68r; *Senato Terra*, 28 June 1458, Reg. 4, fol. 75v; 14 November 1460, Reg. 4, fol. 158v.

8. Dana E. Katz, *The Jewish Ghetto and the Visual Imagination of Early Modern Venice*, Cambridge: Cambridge University Press 2017, 37–38.

from what was programmed. Perhaps the "porosity" in guild practices, in the materiality of the ghetto buildings, i.e. the interstices that existed in between regulations and concrete action, made up the de facto peculiarity of Venice.

The fact is that the word "ghetto" is now used constantly in the media, often referring to cases of physical isolation immensely different from each other, and distant geographically and politically. Today, rethinking the long history of the first ghetto—in Venice—five hundred years after its establishment, its many contradictions, complexity, and the meaning of segregation that this term assumed not only the past, but also in times closer to us as well as, conversely, the closely linked cosmopolitanism, it feels necessary. Knowing this story brings the realization that Jewish identity is an integral part of European identity. Doing so now, twenty-seven years since the fall of the Berlin Wall (1989), in a free and once again unified continent, unable however to govern the new waves of fear triggered by anomalous numbers of immigrants, can perhaps help to meet the challenge that Europe faces to avoid a new season of concrete walls and barbed wire fences to obviate the danger of a world consisting of "an archipelago of ghettos."[9]

---

9. Lucio Caracciolo, "L'arcipelago dei ghetti," *Repubblica* (1 September 2015): 30.

ABBREVIATIONS

AIRE	Archivio dell'IRE (IRE Archive), Venice
AMV	Archivio Municipale (Municipal Archive), Venice
ANP	Archives Nationales (National Archives), Paris
ASU	Archivio Storico (Historical Archive), Udine
ASV	Archivio di Stato (State Archive), Venice
BARM	Biblioteca Renato Maestro (Renato Maestro Library), Venice
BMC	Biblioteca Museo Correr (Correr Museum Library), Venice
BMV	Biblioteca Nazionale Marciana (St. Mark's National Library), Venice

GLOSSARY

ALTANA, ALTANELLE: wooden terraces on wooden poles that extend from the edge of the building; they can be set on the roof or at the water level of a canal.

BAILO: Venetian ambassador or console in Constantinople.

BUCINTORO: state galley (a boat) of the Venice Republic, used for ceremonies, to welcome illustrious guests and, every, year, on the Feast of the Ascension to celebrate the Venetian rite of Marriage of the Sea (*Sposalizio del Mare*), an ancient ceremony symbolizing the maritime dominion of Venice.

CA': house. It has the double meaning of a family home, the place of residence, and the family's entire group of relatives.

CALLE: street (especially in Venice)

CAMPO: in Venice, the quintessential square (*piazza*) is Piazza San Marco. All the other squares are known as *campo* (literally "field" in Italian). The expression is used today, even after they have all been paved. Derivative words such as *campiello*, and *campazzo* designatie smalled, more irregular areas.

CONDOTTA: charter for an agreement between the Republic of Venice and the University of the Jews (*Università degli Ebrei*). The first condotta, based on pawn broking, dates back to 1383 and was signed to last for five years. The charters were then renewed every five years. Starting in 1589, they were renewed every ten years.

CONTRADA: administrative district in Italian cities in the Middle Ages and in the Early Modern times, corresponding more or less to the area of a parish.

FONDACO: government-run warehouse, found in many fifteenth and sixteenth century cities where trade was present. In Venice, they were used for flour or wheat (i.e. the main staples), or by foreigners from a specific country (e.g. Germans, Persians or Turks). They were located along the Grand Canal to allow for unloading and control of the goods by Venetian officials.

FRATERNA: confraternity; a structure used to unify management of funds for assistance (collection and redistribution) and eliminate begging. The University of the Jews created associations of this kind to help orphans, widows and the poor.

LAZZARETTO: island in the Lagoon, where a hospital was set up in 1423, for those stricken with the plague. It was called Lazzaretto Vecchio, perhaps referring to the church of Santa Maria di Nazareth located there, as well as to San Lazzaro, the patron saint of the poor and sick. Starting in 1468 the patients from the island of Lazzaretto Nuovo were also hospitalized there. Instead, Lazzaretto Nuovo was used as a hospice where possibly contagious travelers were quarantined.

LEVANTINE COMMUNITY: the Levantine community groups Jews from Constantinople, Greece and, more generally, from the East.

LIAGÒ: a protrusion from the outside wall of a building, of wood or brick. The element is similar to a covered balcony, often with a window.

SALIZZADA: a cobbled street, paved with flagging.

SCUOLA: Venetian term for religious association recognized by the Republic, with the aim of assistance whose work partly coincided with the trade corporations. In Venice, there were the *Scuole Grandi*, which were names after their patron saint (San Marco, San Giovanni Evangelista, San Rocco), the *Scuole Piccole* and the *Scuole delle Nazioni* (scuole of the Greeks, the Albanians and the Florentines). The synagogues in the ghetto were also known as scuole. In Italian the word means "school".

SESTIERE: the six districts into which Venice was divided (three on each side of the Grand Canal).

STRAZZARIA: trade of second hand objects (clothes, crockery and pots, furniture and textiles), a common occupation among the Jews with the consent of the Republic.

DOMINI DI TERRA FERMA: (literally "mainland domains" or "mainland state"), especially after the fifteenth century, the Venetian Republic ruled over a vast area of the Veneto and today's Lombardy (Padua, Vicenza, Verona, Treviso, Udine, Brescia, and Bergamo). These territories were in contrast with the Domini da Mar ("Domains of the Sea"), which included the Adriatic Coast, the Levant islands and part of Greece.

UNIVERSITÀ DEGLI EBREI OR COMUNITÀ EBRAICA: University of the Jews or Jewish Community. There were different national communities (German, Italian, Levantine and Spanish) and therefore different universities for each national group. The two terms are substantially synonymous. The University of the Jews oversaw problems of internal justice, division of taxes according to each family's economic conditions and, more in general, it took care of public life in the ghetto (roads, wells, illumination, and safety).

VENETIAN OFFICES OR INSTITUTIONS

AVOGADORI DI COMUN: a group of three municipal lawyers who were the guardians of the law and oversaw the legitimacy of the resolutions adopted by the government offices.

CAPI DEI SESTIERI: Guards with the duties of ensuring civil behavior in the city's six sestieri.

COLLEGIO: The *Collegio dei Savi*, or simply the *Collegio*, was created in 1380. It consisted of six members (one from each *sestiere*). Practically speaking, it was the Council of Ministers or executive branch of the Republic. It later came to consist of sixteen members with the expansion of the Venetian dominions.

CONSIGLIO OR MAGGIOR CONSIGLIO: the Great Council was composed by a number of members—changing over time, from 35 in the 12th century to 100 and after the "Serrata" in 1297 many more (the large part of the aristocracy)—with legislative knowledge and deliberation powers.

CONSIGLIO DEI DIECI: the Council of Ten, also known as the Council. It was one of the most important government bodies of the Republic of Venice from 1310 until it fell in 1797. It consisted of ten members and was elected every year by the Great Council for the purpose of overseeing the security of the state.

CONSOLI DEI MERCANTI: four judges charged with deciding between arguing merchants. It convened at the Rialto.

GIUDICI DEL PIOVEGO: the magistrates in charge of the management of public spaces and, especially, the relations and limits between public and private spaces within the city.

GIUDICI DEL PROPRIO: judicial magistracy instituted in 1235, initially with extensive civil and criminal jurisdiction, later reduced with the creation of other magistrates. Its duties included overseeing dowries, wills for real estate, the appointment of executors, the ownership of property formerly held by Venetians who had died outside Venice, divisions and disputes between brothers.

PROCURATORI DI SAN MARCO: Procurators of San Marco. Office of nine members charged with managing San Marco, divided into *Provveditori di San Marco de Supra* (Superintendents of San Marco Above—overseeing the Basilica and Piazza San Marco), *de Citra* (responsible for the side of the city on *that side* of the Grand Canal) and the *de Ultra* (the part of the city on *the other side* of the Grand Canal). The procurators met at the Loggetta del Campanile and lived in the Procuratie in the Piazza San Marco.

PROTO: a technician charged with drawing up projects and budgets. He served under a public magistrate (*Provveditori al Sale*, *Magistrati alle Acque*, *Procuratori di San Marco*). The proto was chosen by a competition and paid monthly.

PROTO AL SALE: technician of the *Provveditori al Sale*, director of urban public works.

PROVVEDITORI ALLE FORTEZZE: Venetian magistrature instituted by the Senate in 1542, as part of the reorganization of the defensive system at the beginning of the century. It dealt with all the problems related to the design, construction, maintenance and supply of state fortresses from the Stato da Tera, (literally "mainland state", the name given to the hinterland territories of the Republic of Venice beyond the Adriatic coast in Northeast Italy) and fortified seaports from the *Stato da Màr* (the State of the Sea, the name given to the Republic of Venice's maritime and overseas possessions).

PROVVEDITORI AL SALE: magistrates in charge of collecting duties on salt. The sums collected were used to finance the refurbishing and maintenance of buildings and public spaces. The proto working under this magistrate was a technician (an engineer or an expert with experience in construction sites).

QUARANTIA CRIMINALE: The *Consiglio dei Quaranta* (Council of Forty) was established at the end of the twelfth or the beginning of the thirteenth century and was active until the fall of the Republic, although its duties changed. It originally had widespread powers, including suggesting laws, with public and governing responsibilities along with the *Maggior Consiglio*. But it was also involved in monetary, financial, administrative, and judicial affairs (and for that reason also of pawn broking).

SAVI ALLE DECIME: Ten member magistracy who collected the "Decima" (property taxes on houses, shops and storerooms based on declarations by the owners). These taxes were also paid by the Jews, even if they never really owned their buildings.

SAVI ED ESECUTORI ALLE ACQUE (or simple SAVI ALLE ACQUE): Experts and Executors of the Waters. Three experts who worked unpaid, appointed by the Senate and in chargeof supervising the public waters of the lagoon and canals, the Republic's most precious assets.

SAVI ALLA MERCANZIA: five member magistracy instituted in 1506, overseeing merchant's activity. They were soon (1541) put in charge of the Ghetto Vecchio and of trade by the Levantine Jews, as well of the German and Turkish warehouses.

SENATO (Senate of the Mare/Senate of the Terra): originally known as the Consiglio dei Pregadi or *Consiglio dei Rogati* (*Pregadi* from the fact that the members were asked to lend their services). It consisted of sixty patricians, elected for a year, whose responsibilities covered foreign policy, trade, navigation, the military, and finances. While there were initially sixty members, later on additional senators were appointed.

SERENISSIMA: literally, the Most Serene Republic of Venice. The expression was first used in the fifteenth century, a mythical reference to the government of the Venetian Republic. The Serenissima included the marine and mainland state, i.e. a vast territory in Dalmatia and the Levant islands on the east and the present day Veneto and part of Lombardy.

UFFICIALI ALLE RAZON VECCHIE: judicial magistacy instituted by the Senate in 1368, composed of three members, with the task of reviewing state accounts and monitoring some levies. Starting in 1385, the Ufficiali alle Razon Vecchie were also debt collectors for all the Republic's debtors.

UFFICIO AL CATTAVER: the magistracy overseeing taxes and smuggling. It therefore was in charge of supervising public assets. After the ghetto was created, its duties including controlling the Jews and their activity, pawnbroking in particular.

ACKNOWLEDGEMENTS

I would like to extend my thanks the following: Elisa Bastianello, Alessandra Ferrighi, Ludovica Galeazzo, Gianmario Guidarelli, Martina Massaro, and Renata Segre for their valuable scientific collaboration, recommendation of certain documents and suggestions; John Caniato, Michela Dal Borgo, Claudia Salmini, Schiavon Alessandra and Director Raffaele Santoro for concrete assistance lent in the State Archives; Alexandre Melissinos for the diligence and accuracy he used in his graphic design and photographic scans; Luke Pilot for the photographs taken in the synagogues and outside the three Ghetti; Michele Luzzatto and Sylvie Mouches for their meticulous passion and dedication to the editorial work; and Barbara Del Mercato for her commitment in keeping contacts with Italian and foreign scholars.

I would also like to thank especially the publisher of the English edition, Marco Jellinek, for his meticulous re-reading of the Italian text, his notes and his pertinent observations. My thanks also go to Lenore Rosenberg Bahbout for her careful attention, the competence she has shown in the subject and the respect with which she translated my words.

Here, we want to express our special affection in recollection of Ennio Concina a dear friend who is no longer with us and, with whom many years ago, I started my studies on the topics covered here and shared unforgettable conversations and thoughts on history, architecture and culture.